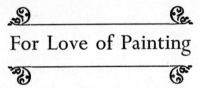

For Love of Painting

For Love of Painting

The Life of Sir Gerald Kelly, K.C.V.O., P.R.A.

DEREK HUDSON

Peter Davies : London

Peter Davies Limited
15 Queen Street, Mayfair, London W1X 8BE
LONDON MELBOURNE TORONTO
JOHANNESBURG AUCKLAND

© Derek Hudson 1975
First published 1975

432 06952 6

Printed in Great Britain by
Richard Clay (The Chaucer Press), Ltd.,
Bungay, Suffolk

Contents

Illustrations

Preface

When Sir Gerald Kelly died in the early days of 1972, aged 92, there were few then living who had known, as he had, Cézanne, Degas, Rodin, W. G. Grace: all dead for more than half a century. But although he outlived most of his contemporaries, Kelly retained to the end his exceptional vitality and passion for great painting.

There are several good reasons for attempting a memoir of him. In Kenneth Clark's view, he was 'the most reliable portrait painter of his time'. Clive Bell thought him 'about the best President of the Royal Academy since Sir Joshua Reynolds', and he organized several of the finest exhibitions ever seen at Burlington House.

Other reasons are, for a biographer, even more compelling. Kelly was not only a famous conversationist and an attractive public speaker; he was also an engaging letter-writer who watched his prose as carefully as the paint on his canvases. Having known the great artists of Europe, from the Impressionists onward, he recorded some of his memories for television, a medium in which he became a star overnight in 1953. Thus, although Kelly never published a book of reminiscences, he left materials 'in his own hand' for his biography; and these can be supplemented by the recollections of those who knew him.

He was, as he often maintained, a happy man who enjoyed life, especially in his own home and studio, a man whose love of art and whose gift for expressing his enthusiasm shaped many people's understanding. Habitually courteous, he was generous to artists in need, and to all who asked his advice.

There was an impatient side to him, of which he was fully aware. 'Kellys are naughty', he used to say. Answering a B.B.C. panel (17 February 1953) which asked him to describe 'what sort of person' he was, he replied: 'Very charming, extremely intelligent, and extremely unpleasant – all mixed up together.' That he was capable of such a self-critical assessment is a measure both of Kelly's integrity and of his essential Irishness.

In a life ranging from the romantically adventurous to the formally conventional, one thing remained constant: Kelly's love of painting. He would come to the rescue of a threatened or neglected masterpiece with the chivalry of a knight towards a damsel in distress. Pursuing the interests of his beloved Royal Academy, pleading for the loan of a

picture, painting an authentic portrait of a great man, he blended
tenacity with charm, craftsmanship with guile. Such fidelity, such
basic civility, such patience from the impatient, deserve to be remembered.

This biography has been compiled from so many and various sources,
among them newspapers and B.B.C. transcripts, that it has not lent
itself to strict documentation. Wherever possible, I have provided
dates and references in the text. I have added a bibliography and some
Notes on Sources which will enable readers to trace the provenance of
other material.

I could not have undertaken the task without the consent and co-
operation of Lady Kelly. My first and most grateful thanks must go to
her. She has been at great pains to help me by the loan of press cuttings,
letters, and other items from her husband's papers; by giving me the
invaluable benefit of her recollections; and by reading and commenting
on my typescript.

Next I must express my indebtedness to the President and Council
of the Royal Academy for permission to use its archives. I am obliged
to Sir Thomas Monnington, P.R.A., for allowing me to quote from
his memorial address; to Mr Sidney C. Hutchison, Secretary of the
Royal Academy, for his encouragement and for reading my typescript;
and to Miss Constance-Anne Parker, Librarian, and her assistant Mrs
Harding, for much practical help.

For enlightenment on Kelly's family background, I am indebted to
Mr R. Duncombe, Company Secretary, Kelly's Directories. Kelly's
association with Eton College, as boy and man, led me to correspond
with Sir Robert Birley, Sir Claude Elliott, Mr F. J. B. Coleridge
(Vice-Provost), Mr M. McCrum (Headmaster), and Mr Jeremy Potter
(College Librarian); all were kind and I remember Mr Potter's hospitality with gratitude. Mr Graham Storey, of Trinity Hall, came to my
aid by throwing light on the Cambridge careers of the Rev. F. F. Kelly
and his son.

Among Kelly's many friends and acquaintances in the art world who
have written to me and given much helpful information and advice, I
would particularly thank Lord Clark, Sir Francis Watson, Sir Anthony
Blunt, Mr Benedict Nicolson, Sir John Rothenstein, Sir Oliver Millar,
Mr Jack Hillier, Mr Dennis Farr, Mr Brian Reade, and Mr H. Andrew
Freeth, R.A.

In addition, there were those who could speak with knowledge of
Kelly's studio practice – notably Mr John Napper, Mrs Heda Berkeley,

and Mr John Frye Bourne, all of whom responded with generosity. Dr R. W. Hilles very kindly allowed me to use his diary of 1930–31 which gives vivid glimpses of a fashionable portrait painter's life. Further enlightenment came from several of Kelly's secretaries, Mrs Pamela McClintock, Miss Lorna Hubbard, Mrs Doreen Kennedy, Mrs Penelope Reid, and Mrs Renee Goldberg.

I owe a special debt to Sir Owen Morshead for wise advice, useful suggestions, and the loan of important material; he illuminated Kelly's life from 1939 onwards, especially the years spent at Windsor Castle during the Second World War. To Sir Alan Lascelles and Sir Martin Charteris I also owe thanks for insights into this period.

At the B.B.C. I have to thank Mr R. D. Hewlett, Head of Reference and Registry Services, while Mr Bill Duncalf and Mr Edward Halliday went to great trouble to help me re-create Kelly's career in television. I am much obliged to Mr Oliver Davies for enabling me to quote from the files of the Royal College of Music and the R.C.M. Magazine.

Others whom I remember thankfully include: Lord Adeane, Mrs Lavender Alers Hankey, Mr Gordon P. Anderson, Mr William A. Barnes, Mrs Rotha Barnfield, Colonel I. R. Burrows, Mr Arthur Calder-Marshall, Mr William A. Coles, Mr Grenville Cook, Sir William Charles Crocker, Mrs Charles Cundall, Mr David Dean, Mrs Mary Delgado, Mr John Dugdale, Miss Sibylle Jane Flowers, Mr James Harding, Sir Rupert Hart-Davis, Mr A. J. Craig Harvey, Miss Margaret Hine, Dr L. Holliday, Mrs E. Hooper, Mr Ellic Howe, Mr C. Jennings, Mrs Anne Knowles, Mr Andrew Leslie of the Leva Gallery, Mr Kenneth E. Pottle, Mr Reginald Pound, Mr Cecil Roberts, the Marqués de Saavedra, Mr R. H. F. Scott, Mr E. C. Shaw, Mrs Valérie Spry, Mrs R. M. Tulloch, Mr W. Van Essen, Sir John Wheeler-Bennett, Mr John Whitehead, Mr Gerald Yorke.

I have to express grateful thanks to the following for specific copyright permissions: the British Broadcasting Corporation, in respect of original copyright in material quoted from their transcripts; Mr Spencer Curtis Brown, literary executor of W. Somerset Maugham, for permission to quote from writings by Maugham and to make a limited use of his letters to Kelly; Mr Romilly John, for letters from Augustus John; Dame Margot Fonteyn de Arias, for a letter; Mr Hugh McLellan, widower of Yvonne Arnaud, for a letter of hers; Mrs Valerie Eliot and Faber and Faber Ltd for letters of T. S. Eliot; Mr Winston S. Churchill and B.T. Publications Ltd, for letters from Sir Winston Churchill.

I must hope for indulgence in respect of a few short quotations. In certain cases I have not known to whom to write, and to some of my inquiries I have received no answers. I apologize for my shortcomings and trust no harm has been done.

The book has benefited greatly from the wise editorial suggestions of Derek Priestley.

Finally, let me thank Mrs Margery Long-Fox for the typing of my manuscript, and Mr Douglas Matthews for preparing the Index.

Hindhead, 1974.   D.H.

CHAPTER ONE

Ancestry and Education

STEPHEN BLACK: And where were you born?
GERALD KELLY: In London – in Paddington.
BLACK: But you are of Irish extraction . . .
KELLY: Oh yes – completely.
BLACK: Both your parents were Irish?
KELLY: Yes. My Mother was half. My father was whole.

'Frankly Speaking', Home
Service, B.B.C., 6 May 1953.

I

Gerald Kelly's Irish ancestry can be traced back to the tenth century, and to Keallach, Chief of Hy-Many, whose great-grandson Teige 'Cata-Briam' was killed fighting the Danes at the battle of Clontarf in 1014. Other distant forebears were Conor O'Kelly, who is said to have built O'Kelly's church at Clonmacnoise in 1167, and William Boy O'Kelly, who built Callow Castle and founded the Abbey of Kilconnell. The latter gave a famous feast at Gaille at Christmas, 1351, to 'the Poetts, brehons, bardes, harpers, gamesters, and jesters'.

The Kellys from whom Gerald immediately descended came from the Galway border of Roscommon. But his great-grandfather Festus Kelly was a Captain in the 96th Regiment, living in London, and his grandfather Festus Frederick was appointed by the Postmaster-General in 1837 to the office of Her Majesty's Inspector of Letter Carriers. He it was who established the fortunes of his English family and gave his name to Kelly's Directories.

The production of a London street directory of names and addresses had been sporadic since the end of the seventeenth century. From 1799 onwards the compilation of new directories was entrusted by the Post

Office to the Inspectors of Letter Carriers, who relied on the information of the carriers and were allowed to keep the profits. F. F. Kelly purchased the copyright from the widow of his predecessor. After he took over, changes were made. In 1840–41, a trades section and a streets section were added; and the book began to be printed by William Kelly and Co., a firm of which his brother William was the head. When the employment of letter carriers on the directory was attacked in parliament, F. F. Kelly engaged his own staff; by 1854 the book was being formally produced by Kelly and Co.

During the next forty years, various other specialized directories were developed by the firm, and in 1894 the business was consolidated under the name Kelly's Directories Ltd. By the time of the founder's death in 1883, his eldest son having meanwhile been ordained a clergyman of the Church of England, he was succeeded in the firm by a nephew and then by a great-nephew, though the founder's family retained a considerable interest.* The founder had, incidentally, laid down a fine cellar of wine.

The Inspector of Letter Carriers was married to Harriet, daughter of John Richards, who had homes in London and Brighton. The couple lived in Bedford Square, Bloomsbury. Their eldest son, born in 1838, received the same names as his father, but used them in the reverse order: Frederic Festus. He went to Eton, where he learned to row. After matriculating at Trinity, Cambridge, he migrated to Trinity Hall in 1857. There he distinguished himself as a scholar and athlete. An all-round sportsman, he rowed bow in the Trinity Hall Lents boat that went head of the river in 1859. But the historian of the boat club adds: 'his chief claim upon the gratitude of his College is that to him more than to anyone is due the formation of the Trinity Hall Association' which 'has been of incalculable value in keeping old Hall men in touch with one another and with the College'.

Leslie Stephen was a tutor, a clergyman, and the main rowing coach when Frederic Kelly went up to Trinity Hall. Kelly admitted his influence: 'It was Leslie Stephen who did the "making" of our and the next generation of undergraduates.' He obtained a second class in the LL.B in 1860 and took the LL.M. in 1863. He was admitted to the Inner Temple. His father sent him on a European tour, expecting him to return to a legal career. Instead, he decided to go into the Church: another example, perhaps, of Stephen's influence, though the latter eventually abandoned holy orders.

* In 1921 control passed to the Amalgamated Press, and in the nineteen-fifties to the International Publishing Corporation.

Frederic Kelly was ordained deacon in 1861 and priest in 1862. He held curacies at Hilton, Huntingdonshire; Stockport, Cheshire; and in Kensington in London, before he became curate of St Michael's, Paddington, in 1871. Two years later, he married Blanche, daughter of Robert Bradford, a man of means who lived at Franks, Farningham, Kent. Their first two children were girls, Rose Edith and Eleanor Constance Mary. On 9 April 1879 their only son was born at 78 Cambridge Terrace, Paddington, on the east side of Regent's Park, and was given the names Gerald Festus.

Gerald arrived in the borough of Paddington, where he was to live for most of his life; but he left it in 1880 for Camberwell Vicarage, when his grandfather bought for the Paddington curate the living of the parish of St Giles. Frederic Kelly was to serve his Camberwell parishioners loyally and successfully for thirty-five years. His younger brother, John Richard Kelly, was, incidentally, M.P. for North Camberwell, 1886–92; so 'Kelly of Camberwell' had some significance.

2

The Vicar's chief gifts to his son seem to have been abundant nervous energy, a gift for conscientious organization and exposition, and an irascible Irish charm. Life at Camberwell Vicarage was generally happy but had its difficulties. 'Monday was pretty grim,' said Gerald Kelly in a radio interview in 1953, for it was the day on which his father recovered from his Sunday duties. 'If the children were kept out of his way on Monday, things went very well.'

The same radio programme provided Gerald's earliest memory:

> I remember being dressed in a blue frock, smocked with pale yellow, and being stood on the end of one of those curious, hideous sofas that people used to have at the bottom of beds. A thing like a sort of slug. And I was stood on the top end while this yellow, yellow dress was adjusted, and, why I do not know, but I kicked my mother in the face, and I was beaten by my father, and I rushed away and spent the rest of the day under a bath.

The episode may suggest an early manifestation of artistic or aesthetic intuition. It does not represent Gerald's opinion of his dignified good-humoured mother, a typically Victorian lady in character and deportment who spoiled her only son and whom he loved (Plate 4). He admitted, nevertheless, that he could not paint her portrait, because she looked at him with such intense affection that it put him off. He painted his father more than once, notably in 'The Vicar in his Study' (Plate 2), one of his masterpieces. Once he had accepted the idea of Gerald becoming an artist, his father greatly encouraged him, and indeed kept a careful record of his early works and exhibitions.

The father's influence was stronger than the mother's, but did not make a churchman of Gerald Kelly. However, when asked whether he considered himself a religious man, he replied: 'Put me in front of a Rembrandt, and I can answer.'

The church of St Giles, Camberwell, which Gerald attended so often as a boy – the experience may have exhausted his capacity for churchgoing – is a lofty, impressive building, consecrated in 1844, and designed by George Gilbert Scott to replace an earlier church which had been burned to the ground. When Gerald was young, the gloom of the interior may have predisposed his eye to the low tones of Whistler and Pryde. Now, in 1973, the church has light and space. Most of the dark stained glass has been replaced by plain glass, and the galleries, with their iron columns on both sides of the nave, have disappeared; they became unsafe owing to bomb damage in the Second World War.

The Vicarage opposite the church was pulled down in the nineteen-sixties after a century of existence, to be replaced by buildings more suited to the needs of the modern parish. It had been a huge house, standing in an acre of garden, with three floors over a basement, topped by high Victorian gables. There were a large hall and about eighteen big rooms; one of these was Gerald Kelly's studio until he was past thirty.

It was a wealthy living. The Vicar's stipend had been increased from the rents of houses built when part of the very large vicarage garden had been sold about 1860. No wonder that the Rev. F. F. Kelly was willing to stay for thirty-five years. But the work was anything but a sinecure. In his early days he often presided over Camberwell Vestry, and, so long as he was vicar, he was chairman of Wilson's Grammar School, which he succeeded in re-establishing in 1882. It was probably as an educationist that his parishioners knew him best. The only publication he acknowledged was an improving book for children: *Sermons on Plain Duties*. This emphasis on training and discipline links him with Gerald Kelly's care for his studio assistants and for the students of the Royal Academy schools.

Gerald owed his father a further debt – for inspiring his life-long love of cricket. Though at one time an occasional golfer, he was not in general a sportsman; yet watching cricket became something special for him. He set down his thoughts on the game in a typescript written in 1966. He was glad then to be able to follow cricket on television. He said that he had seen all the great batsmen of his time, and that his favourites were Woolley, Hammond, and Hobbs. He thought it was 'more fun when I was younger; there were fewer people who talked about it, and the newspapers weren't full of superior and intelligent articles all about something which isn't very easily described'. But Camberwell Vicarage was at the centre of his cricket memories, and he wrote:

It was in the early nineties, when I was about ten or eleven, that I began to take an interest in cricket. One morning I was mucking about in the hall, and I saw the shadows through the front door of two men, and I found an old clergyman accompanied by the most beautiful young man, and beauty has always thrilled me, even when I was small. The clergyman said, 'Can I see your father?' and I said that I'd see, and in fear and trembling I went to my father's study, and said, 'There's a clergyman to see you,' and then the clergyman slipped by me and said, 'Hello, Mike,' and my father changed and said, 'Hello, Sniffkins,' and they smashed each other on the shoulder blades, and it was all very exciting. Then the clergyman said, 'Charles, this is Mr Kelly, and if there had been blues in his day, he would have done as well as you,' and then the blinding light came, and I knew it was Charles Fry. That is how I really, really, started my career as a cricket fan, and if at that moment the Archangel Gabriel had popped in he would have been a flop.

Then something far more significant happened. My father decided to take me to see a Gentlemen and Players match at Lords. After a very long bus ride we arrived and everybody seemed to know my father and obviously liked him and it was quite wonderful, and then we went to the Pavilion, where I was taken up to the great big man with the black beard, and I was introduced to Dr Grace. Then the Players won the toss and batted all day and Shrewsbury did very nicely, and I thought Gunn was miraculously graceful. When we drove home, Father said to me, 'Never mind, tomorrow we shall be seeing Dr Grace' and we went back, but Grace only made three or four runs, and then he was out, and when he came in to bat again he did no better, and it was all very disappointing. On the long bus journey home, Father didn't look at me, and I didn't look at Father, and then he said to me, 'Well,

Gerald, now you know something. Even Dr Grace doesn't make a hundred every time he goes in to bat.' Do you know, that remark has controlled my whole life, it has influenced me in my job. One doesn't often make a hundred.

The Kellys had as their neighbour in the Peckham Road, a pioneer Australian cricketer in Dr (later Sir) David Serjeant. There are stories that Gerald at one time flirted with his daughter Cora, and his sister Rose with one of his sons.

Although he had a close alliance with his father, Gerald's early life was greatly influenced by his mother, his two elder sisters, and their nurse. He acknowledged later that he was a spoiled little boy. An anecdote about Miss Bird, the Kellys' nurse-governess, tends to bear this out. She took Gerald on a walk to Dulwich College Picture Gallery when he was nine. They went over Grove Lane, a considerable incline, and at the top Gerald detached himself from Miss Bird's care and engaged in 'acrobatic handstands'. As Gerald was a delicate, indeed sickly child, she feared for his health; but like Father William he did it 'again and again'. There was usually, however, throughout his life a compensatory aspect to Gerald's displays of naughtiness. These early visits gave him a lasting interest in the Dulwich pictures. When, more than fifty years later, the opportunity came for him to serve the Gallery, he was not only willing but eager.

3

Gerald went to Eton in the Michaelmas term, 1892. Philip Williams was his housemaster, first at Gulliver's, then at Hawtrey's, a house centrally placed on the High Street, opposite the chapel – a situation comparable to the Kellys' at Camberwell Vicarage. His tutors were John Cole and later R. P. L. Booker, 'the ambassador of happiness', as Hubert Brinton wrote of him after his death.

Gerald's feelings about Eton were mixed. When asked in a B.B.C. interview whether he had enjoyed himself, he replied 'Not awfully.' But he told the same questioners: 'At Eton one was left entirely alone. One had a room of one's own, and I think that is why I got early into the habit of thinking for myself.'

On the same occasion he said that at Eton he had no interest in art. This he contradicted afterwards, and it was not strictly true, for he was soon showing talent in watercolour sketching; a drawing of Windsor

Castle, for example (Plate 1b) is dated April 1897. What he seems to have meant was that his artistic tastes in his teens were not assertive or affected. In a talk to Eton boys delivered in later life, he pleaded for sincerity of opinion. 'When I was a young man, not to admire good art was considered the most natural thing to do,' he said, but it had acquired a social stigma which he deprecated: 'I don't believe that everybody likes Cézanne. I don't believe that everybody admires T. S. Eliot.' He continued:

> When I was at Eton, people were very uncultured. We who were interested in the arts were rather snubbed. It was considered not very manly. We had to keep our aesthetic emotions well under control. Lowbrows controlled public opinion. Looking back over my life, I think one is happier in a society controlled by lowbrows than a society controlled by Bloomsbury and all that Bloomsbury stands for.

Gerald had none of his father's skills at games; and his academic progress at the school was regular rather than spectacular. He began in the Upper Fourth, passed through the Remove and the Lower and Middle Fifths, and ended in the Upper Fifth. Despite this unexciting career, he was very proud in retrospect of having been at Eton; he habitually wore his Old Etonian tie, and when he became President of the Royal Academy – the first Etonian to do so – he ventured to ask the Headmaster, in May 1950, for a whole holiday for the school.

In his letter he wrote: 'I hope it is not that I am suffering from a swollen head, but I am wondering whether it would be possible for me to fulfil an ambition so vast, so ridiculous, that it has lain forgotten in my mind ever since I was a Lower boy.' He recalled that somebody had then asked 'for a whole holiday because something great had happened', and that the boon had been granted, and that he had said to himself: 'That is a thing, my boy, that you will never be able to do.'

The conclusion was accurate, as far as Gerald Kelly's request was concerned, for it was refused on principle. But he was allowed to present to the art collection his oil painting of Upper School after the bombing of 1940, and he is remembered for his portraits of two Provosts, one in College Hall of Dr M. R. James, seen standing against a background of books; the other of his friend Sir Henry Marten, which hangs in the Marten Library.

4

'I really do believe that I am the luckiest man that I have ever known,' Kelly said on television in 1956. 'By luck, I mean that providence is constantly interfering on my behalf and things that have happened to me have very rarely been the result of my intention, and things have turned out marvellously well, marvellously well.'

Providence intervened in the autumn term of 1895 by giving Gerald an abscess on the liver. He was seriously ill and had to be removed from Eton. The doctor recommended that he should go on a voyage to Cape Town and spend the following winter there. (As Kelly said he was seventeen when he went to South Africa, this must have been in 1896.)

His pretty sister Rose (Plate 3) came out with him and flirted with most of the eligible men on board the ship. Her brother shared a cabin with a young architect named Macey who was attracted to Rose. Gerald believed that his sister's admirer tried to win his support; he praised the boy's watercolours and told him that he ought to become an artist and study in Paris. After they arrived in Cape Town, the architect called several times at the Kellys' hotel. Eventually he proposed to Rose, but she turned him down. They did not see any more of him after that.

The episode had, however, left a lasting mark on Gerald's impressionable mind. In particular, the idea of studying art in Paris preoccupied him. When, with his sister, he returned to Camberwell Vicarage, much improved in health, he announced to his father that he intended to become a painter. He described his father's reaction in one of his autobiographical television programmes:

> My father was a very simple man. He said 'rot', and I said 'No, no, Mr Macey said I had real . . . tremendous talent'. My father said 'Nonsense, no member of my family has ever shown the slightest talent – as for your mother's family, they are more or less inane, the whole lot of them.' Well, my mother made a point of disagreeing with my father on a good many things and her only son had to be supported, and the battle waged for six months, at the end of which time my father capitulated and we made a gentleman's agreement. If I would go to Cambridge, which is what he had planned, as he had gone to Cambridge – he went to Eton and Trinity Hall, I was to go to Eton and Trinity Hall – if I promised to fill up that part of the programme, I should be allowed to be a painter.

Kelly matriculated at Trinity Hall at Michaelmas, 1897. He had no
idea of pursuing a regular course of study, and maintained that his only
ambition was to acquire an aegrotat in Botany, an ambition that was
thwarted because no one was taking the Botanical Tripos that year.
However, his father's reputation as a scholar–athlete made his son
welcome in the college, and in particular he attracted the notice of
'an adorable old man', a History Don. This must have been Thomas
Thornely, who soon found that his protégé had no taste for history,
but put him on to reading poetry instead. 'And for three years,'
declared Kelly, 'in a desultory way I read Poetry, under his kindly help,
and it was the most valuable thing that anybody can have. You know,
if you haven't read Poetry before you're twenty-one, you'll never read
it. But if you've read it, a lot of it, as I had, I've read Poetry all my
life.'

Although he only took a Poll degree, Kelly's study of poetry did have
one unusual result – he won the Winchester Reading Prize. This
achievement involves reciting in public passages in classical English
prose and poetry; in the Old Testament and the New Testament and
the English Liturgy; and from a work of some standard divine. It was
useful training for the speechmaking and broadcasting of his later
life.

As with Eton, Kelly retained a positive, if qualified, affection for
Trinity Hall, and when he was eighty he gave a fascinating talk to a
college society on the French Impressionists he had known. Two of his
best portraits, of Dr Henry Bond, Master of the college, and of Lord
Chancellor Maugham, hang in the college hall. He was annoyed at the
condition of the Bond portrait when he examined it in 1957, and
complained to the Master (Sir William Ivor Jennings):

> . . . I was very pleased when I saw the Freddie Maugham. It is, I
> think, a very good Kelly, it has a charming frame and it looked very
> nice . . . I then crossed to look at my portrait of Dr Bond and for
> a few minutes I was very angry indeed.
>
> It has been hanging above a side table where vegetables are
> served and the greasy steam from innumerable cabbages and
> Brussels sprouts has covered its poor surface, which is now greasy
> and growing some kind of mould and the varnish has vitrified and
> gone white. A little to the right of where the unfortunate Dr
> Bond is hanging is a portrait of Sir Henry Maine in an equally
> disgraceful condition. . . .
>
> So if you will ask your people to let the Academy collect Dr

Bond at the same time they collect Lord Maugham*, I will amuse myself removing the growths, scraping off the residue of Brussels sprouts and doing the best I can to restore Dr Bond to the condition it was in when delivered to one of your predecessors. . . .

Dr Bond will then return to you looking its poor best and a new generation can settle down to the job of getting it again properly kippered for use in our hall. (11 July 1957.)

5

One of the most significant, though not the most propitious, meetings of Kelly's undergraduate years was with Aleister Crowley, poet, occultist, first-class mountaineer, and a chess-player who won his half-blue for the university. Long before his death in 1947, Crowley was to become a notorious symbol of decadence, evil, and Satanic indulgence; but as a handsome young man at Trinity, with a floppy bow-tie and pure silk shirts, he must have had attractions, for he was an impressive talker with considerable panache; the perverted magician had not yet taken control.

Clifford Bax vividly described a meeting with Crowley at St Moritz, a few years later:

> A powerful man, with black magnetic eyes, walked up to me. He wore a velvet coat with ermine lapels, a coloured waistcoat, silk knee-breeches, and black silk stockings. He smoked a colossal meerschaum . . . Every evening we played chess together and to play chess with a man is to realize the voltage of his intellect. A strong and imaginative mind directed the pieces that opposed me. . . .

Kelly heard of Crowley at a Cambridge bookseller's in the May term of 1898, when he was shown a copy of his first volume of poetry, *Aceldama*. His inquiries led to an invitation to Crowley's luxurious book-lined rooms in Trinity Street. The young men had something in common; both came from well-to-do families and were in reaction against clerical fathers. Crowley made an impression on Kelly, who was four years younger; he might have had a very bad influence indeed on a man of lesser integrity and independence.

* The two portraits were to be shown in the 1957 exhibition of Kelly's works in the Diploma Gallery at the Royal Academy.

As it was, Crowley was reduced to writing sarcastically of Kelly in the nineteen-twenties, after he had been elected A.R.A.:

> It saddens me more than I can say to think of that young life which opened with such brilliant promise, gradually sinking into the slough of respectability . . . For he completely hypnotized me into thinking that he had something in him. I took his determination to become an artist as evidence of some trace of capacity and I still hope that his years of unremitting devotion to a hopeless ambition will earn him the right to reincarnate with some sort of soul.

Those lines were written in the knowledge of an irreconcilable quarrel; for Crowley was to have a shattering impact on the Kellys of Camberwell Vicarage.

It was as an undergraduate that Kelly first began to take a serious interest in pictures. He set down some memories of the year 1899:

> . . . Especially I remember the Rembrandt Exhibition in the Royal Academy, which I did not appreciate as much as I loved the commemorative exhibition of the late Sir Edward Burne-Jones.
>
> It amuses me to remember that on the first day of that vacation, knowing that there were two exhibitions, I came up from my father's vicarage of St Giles, Camberwell, on the 'Times' Omnibus and spent an intoxicated morning in the New Gallery in the 'land of clear colours and stories, the region of shadowless hours'. Then I had lunch at the Haymarket Stores (sausages and mashed – you know what undergraduates are) and in the afternoon I went to the Royal Academy Rembrandts. I could not afford a season ticket for both, so I returned to the New Gallery and bought a season ticket for the Burne-Jones, and went regularly twice a week, I should think. I only went to the Rembrandts twice. (Letter to Charles F. Bell, 3 April 1951.)

There is some evidence that Kelly briefly considered the idea of going on to the stage. His cousin Francis Toye in his autobiography gives a glimpse of him in this theatrical phase. Toye records that while he was at Winchester (between 1896 and 1902) he visited the Vicarage, Camberwell, 'primarily to go and see "The Geisha" . . . I remember Gerald's impassioned but analytical praises of Marie Tempest's performance in that charming musical comedy striking me at the time as incredibly sophisticated. But Gerald must have been strong meat even then; a friendship of quite uncousinly warmth contracted in later years entitles me to speak with some assurance on that score. . . .'

CHAPTER TWO

Arrival in Paris

I

An important factor in persuading the Vicar of Camberwell to send his son to Paris to study art and painting was the advice of William Dalton, who became Principal of Camberwell School of Arts and Crafts in 1900. Dalton's daughter Mrs Barnfield told the present writer that the Vicar showed her father a collection of Gerald's drawings, and that, after examining them with care, Dalton proclaimed emphatically: 'Let your son go to Paris, you will never regret it.'

The stimulating artistic life of Paris at the turn of the century provided just the incentive and excitement that Kelly needed to inspire him in his chosen career. 'When I got to Paris, something went bang inside me,' he said on television in 1956, 'and I, who had never gone to lectures or ever worked, had been utterly lazy, started to paint. I painted as long as the light lasted and, by and large, I have done that ever since.' It was still the Paris of the Impressionists – 'a city', in the words of Clive Bell, 'of horse-omnibuses and yellow *fiacres* and drivers with shiny white "toppers" . . . of good living and low prices.'

Kelly arrived in Paris alone in 1901, and put up at a hotel opposite the Gare du Nord, being attracted by its name, Hôtel de l'Univers et du Portugal. Thereafter he was often there for short visits. He was soon joined by his sister Rose, who had been married meanwhile to a much older man, Major Skerrett, and left a widow after two years; she stayed with her brother for six months. Kelly acquired a large studio in Montparnasse, looking out on to the Rue Campagne-Première, 'that long romantic stable yard', as Clive Bell called it.

A letter of introduction from a cousin was Kelly's passport to the home of Paul Durand-Ruel, the great art-dealer, who became a most helpful friend. He was invited to dine in the Rue de Rome. Kelly described this as 'one of the greatest moments of my life'. His French was weak, he was nervous when placed next to his hostess at dinner, but he soon forgot his shyness after noticing a small picture on the opposite wall. He stared until Mme Durand-Ruel said 'I think you would enjoy your dinner better if you got up and had a look at it.' The picture was 'At the Races' by Degas, an instant revelation to Kelly.

After dinner, his host showed him the other pictures in his home, including Renoir's portrait of his daughter, which hung in her bedroom, over her bed. In another bedroom was a Renoir portrait of a dancer. Kelly said that, when he left, he 'wasn't quite sane'; Durand-Ruel smiled as he thanked him and said, 'No, no, you must come and see me in the Rue Lafitte, and I will show you a lot.'

Kelly went the next morning to the gallery, the first of many visits. On that occasion he remembered seeing a portrait by Manet of his wife (a picture bought shortly afterwards by George Moore, who became a friend of Kelly's); a picture by Renoir called 'L'Ingénue', which was owned for a time by Blanche Marchesi, the singer; and Monet's landscape 'The Beach at St Adresse'. The impressionists and their followers had a remarkable effect on Kelly. His deepest admiration, however, was always given to Velasquez; after Velasquez, perhaps the chief influence on him was Ingres.

In the television series in which he recalled these memories of his life in Paris, Kelly admitted he was a snob: 'The best is good enough for me, but only just.' He told Durand-Ruel that he longed to meet these great painters, but for some time nothing came of his hints. Then one day Durand-Ruel announced that he was shortly going to visit Claude Monet at Giverny, when his garden was in flower. Now, if Kelly knew enough about gardening to make some interesting remarks to Monet, he might take him with him. As a result, Kelly spent the whole of a ten-day holiday in England studying gardening. 'I think that I can do you honour with any gardener you are likely to present me to,' he reported to Durand-Ruel on his return to Paris. And so they paid the promised visit, which Kelly described as follows:

. . . When we got to Monet's house in Giverny, I looked at the garden and I saw that in fact the joke really was on me. It wasn't a garden that required any scholarship or knowledge. It was nice and large and it was entirely covered with rambling crimson roses which, you know, you get practically speaking in any suburban garden all over England. And there was a little piece of water where there were some common or garden water lilies, and there were some iris, and all my carefully acquired erudition was worth exactly nothing.

But Monet was there, splendid creature, frightfully handsome, huge beard, ever so high, ever so tall, and beautiful daughters, oodles of them. I mean, quite a lot, a brood. And he and Durand-Ruel, of course, were very old friends and I was allowed to wander about. I sort of tried to see into the studio . . . and Monet said, 'No, no, come out into the garden. You must see my flowers, they are lovely.' And it was one of those grey days which are not very interesting, at least I don't think so. And Monet said, '*Le temps, c'est parfait*' – 'It is perfect for looking at flowers, grey day you know, the sun is the ruination of flowers, they look so bright you can't see them, but on a nice grey day like this you can really enjoy the flowers, so come along.' And I started praying to Almighty God, and I said, 'Send the sun, let the sun come out', and do you know, in a very short time it did, and Monet said, 'Here's the sun, let's go back to the studio.'

And so we went back into the studio. And I was very happy and he showed me a lot of pictures. Gosh, some of them were beauty! A great many of them I didn't awfully like. It was when he was in one of those periods, well never mind, it doesn't matter.

I watched him, I listened to him, and then I began talking to one of the daughters, and she said to me that when father was in the mood and things were going well, she had a pretty grim time. In the early morning she charged a wheelbarrow with about a dozen canvases and she trundled it out to the place where he was painting, and would offer one of the pictures – each one of the pictures had a time marked on it – and at 9 o'clock she put the 9 o'clock picture on the easel. And Monet looked at it and said, 'All the light's wrong, and that cloud oughtn't to be up there', and he would get very angry and put the 9 o'clock picture back and say 'Give me the quarter to ten one.' And so they went to some other little place quite close . . . and if everything was right it was splendid, he worked and worked, and he was happy. But if the light was wrong, he was very irritable indeed.'

2

Kelly pestered Durand-Ruel for a long time to be allowed to meet Edgar Degas. The meeting came about unexpectedly. He was enjoying a collection of forty Renoirs, which the dealer had assembled in his gallery with the object of selling them in America, 'when the door opened and in came a gay young man, older than myself of course, English, with a lot of reddish brown hair, and he said "I am sorry to intrude, but they told me downstairs that you were up here looking at the Renoirs and I thought you wouldn't mind my coming up too, my name is Walter Sickert." '

The artists appreciated each other's company, and Kelly soon heard Sickert suggesting, to his delight, that he should take him to see Degas. 'I know him very well and he'll like you.'

Kelly's first impression of Degas, when they had climbed to the top of a house in the Rue Victor Massey, was that he was a 'funny little man – rather irritable – and he obviously didn't like the sight of me'. Things did not get much better when they moved into 'the most untidy studio into which I had ever been in my life'. Degas pulled out one of his portfolios at random, and it contained about forty drawings of a woman scratching her armpit. 'They were always frightfully interesting,' said Kelly loyally, 'because you *saw* the scratching . . . I didn't think that meeting Degas would be just one long conversation all about a woman scratching her armpit . . . But that is what it had really turned out to be.'

However, their acquaintance proved more rewarding than might have been feared, and after the first visit Kelly was able to think of Degas as 'a nice little man'. He received an invitation to call again, and did so two or three times a year for many years. He confessed that he could not 'remember one visit from another'. Degas rarely showed him his own pictures: 'he really liked to show you the pictures he had bought that were other people's'.

These disappointing reminiscences of Degas were not thought adequate for transmission after Kelly had prepared them for television. His memories of Auguste Rodin were much more copious, and were only with difficulty compressed into two fifteen-minute programmes. Again, he owed the introduction to Durand-Ruel: 'I want to send a letter over to Auguste Rodin,' said the dealer, 'Will you take it for me?' Kelly replied: 'Yes, rather.' The story may be continued in his own words:

> So I went to the Rue de l'Université where he had three studios and I went in and there he was, with a marvellous beard, splendid, he was one of the most marvellous, magnificent heads I have ever seen, and he received the letter, and it was a long letter, and he said, 'Just wait a moment while I read it through, and look at anything you like.' And I looked – there were a lot of pedestals,

and on each pedestal there was a figure, and I looked at several of them, and then one was so sweet I patted it, and he came over and said 'You like that?' and I said, 'Yes, indeed I do.' And he looked at it and said, 'Yes, it is good, isn't it?' And he patted her. So I patted another part of her, and we both patted this young lady, and then he showed me another one, and it was awfully good of him because obviously Durand-Ruel had said be nice to this young man, and he was being most awfully nice.

Kelly saw a lot of Rodin, whose advice and kindness he greatly valued.* He also became very fond of Madame Rodin, visited them frequently in Paris, and was invited down to Meudon. He spent most of one day at Meudon helping to arrange the plaster casts of three muses who were intended to set off Rodin's heroic statue of Victor Hugo. '. . . I worked and sweated all through that morning while these women were moved about by these cranes. And as far as I know, no great progress was made; the old master said, "*C'est affreux, changez tout.*" And so we swung these women about, and we put them in other positions, and during the whole of that day, as I say, we moved them, and I don't believe any progress was made, but I did stay to lunch.' The muses were never included in the design, because Rodin could not get them right, and so the statue now stands alone.

In return for the friendship of Rodin, whom he called the 'most splendid figure that I have ever known' and 'the greatest sculptor of my time', Kelly was able to do him a good turn by persuading a wealthy American woman to buy several of his works – and this at a time when Rodin was hard up, because the City of Paris had refused to accept his statue of Balzac. Rodin thanked Kelly by saying, 'You deserve something, choose anything you like'; and so Kelly became the owner of two pieces from the master's studio.

When Rodin was appointed President of the International Society after Whistler's death in 1903, he paid a visit to London. His pupil John Tweed and Kelly accompanied him. It fell to them to act as interpreters, and to guide Rodin through a reception accorded him at the British Museum. Having at last persuaded the distinguished officials to leave him alone, they were rewarded by seeing Rodin kiss the nose of a sculptured horse.

* Rodin was in touch with Kelly's father and wrote to him in 1903 commending his son's artistic talents, saying '*il porte le sentiment plus profondement loin que l'on ne fait d'habitude*'. (Sotheby's Catalogue, 12 March 1974, Lot 360.)

3

Another sculptor for whom Kelly had a great admiration was Aristide
Maillol, and he made a journey to see him in his country home:

> *.* . . I have forgotten where it was, we went in a train, of
> course – and we arrived and we went into a not very impressive,
> vast studio, rather like a barn, and I was presented to M. Maillol,
> who was a little man, with a magnificent head. His eyes were
> rather close together but he had a long straight pointed nose – an
> aggressive nose – and a beard, lots of beard, and fine eyebrows. I
> like eyebrows – fine eyebrows – and he looked as if he was a Greek
> – he looked as if he might have just stepped off one of the pedi-
> ments of a Greek theatre, a temple.

Maillol spent some time complaining to Kelly's companion of the
cost of making moulds; then he talked to Kelly about his artistic
methods – he specialized in the female nude – and explained how
useful his wife (or housekeeper?) Clothilde was to him when he was in
difficulties. Maillol said:

> '*Quelques fois je me perds*' – 'Sometimes I lose the way' – '*Qu'est-ce
> que je fais?*' – and then he suited his actions to the word. 'What do
> I do? – I go to the door – *Je l'ouvre*' – and he opened the door . . .
> '*Je l'ouvre et j'appelle* "Clothilde!"' Well, there was a silence and
> that shout echoed and then her footsteps – '*Elle vient* – She comes'.
> And dammit all, in the doorway there was Clothilde, a most
> magnificent woman . . . She stood there, smiling, and he went
> dramatically back and he said to me, '*Elle vient, qu'est-ce que je fais*
> – What do I do?' . . . And he stooped down and picked up her
> skirt, he just tranquilly raised it up above her head, and there you
> saw her admirable legs, of a massive construction, covered with
> hand-knitted stockings, which stopped a little way above the knee
> with great garters, and then above that there rose her red mottled,
> splendid thighs.
> And then he said this beautiful thing, '*Et je retrouve le marbre* – I
> find the marble again' . . . 'You see, sometimes I lose the way,
> I send for Clothilde, I look at her, I raise her skirt, I see her, and I
> find the marble again' . . .
> Meanwhile, there was Clothilde standing there, and after a

minute or two, when I had regarded her person, as much as I could see of it, with respect and admiration, the old man dropped her skirt and she stood there smiling. Of course, he must have done it often, it must have been a wheeze of his, and then she said to me, 'Lunch will be ready in a very little while.' And it was an admirable lunch. And I sat next to Clothilde and she told me what a funny old boy he was. She had started life in a factory he had for embroidery, and then he had fallen in love with her, and whether they were actually married or not, I don't know, but she was worth a packet to him. All French artists seem to provide themselves with admirable women. . . .

4

During his early years in Paris, Kelly had a slight acquaintance with Pierre-Auguste Renoir, who left for the south of France in 1904. 'I remember talking to him about gout,' Kelly told *The Times* (18 March 1969); 'I'm of Irish blood, you know, and apparently in France they imagined that Ireland, being damp, was full of people with gout.' Renoir became crippled with arthritis in his later life.

Kelly's only meeting with Paul Cézanne took place when Cézanne was about sixty-five, in 1904 or 1905, shortly before his death. With one or two fellow artists, Kelly went to Aix-en-Provence in the summer, to see some pictures in the museum there. Then one of his friends suggested they should call on Cézanne, whom none of them knew. 'He was wildly admired by twenty or thirty or forty people,' said Kelly fifty years later, 'and really I don't think there were many more – and most of them were painters.' At the post office, where they asked for his address, they were told that M. Cézanne was dead, but the deceased proved to be the artist's father. Finally, they were given an address, a long way away, and set off.

But we got there and it was a scruffy little house and we rang at the door and, well, if I remember rightly, it was an unimportant little garden, and a sort of little servant, a slatty little servant, came out, and we said what we wanted and she slammed the door in our faces and went away. And we went on banging, and after a while Cézanne came out, a little man, as I remember him – very little indeed – with a beret on his head, and grey, and he didn't like it at all. He gave the awful impression he was frightened, he thought we had come to tar and feather him, or something like that. And anyway he took us into the studio, and had I known then how valuable the pictures were going to prove . . . and had I known what an important figure Cézanne was going to make in the world's history, I should have listened with much more attention than I did . . . I only remember one thing . . . He showed us what I thought was a perfectly beastly picture* . . . a huge thing . . . women rather like trees, and the trees rather like women. Very large, very miserable, and sold for a fabulous sum of money.

. . . Well, they went on talking, and obviously the old man didn't want us at all, and I went away into the corner, and saw a little picture which I took up into my hands . . . it represented about three apples, it was so thickly painted that it was like putty. I mean, absolutely loaded with paint, and in the middle of each apple there was a little hole, and round each apple there was a line traced with compasses. He had obviously dug one end of the compasses into the middle of the apple and winkled it round each a bit, and so there was a kind of little ditch in each . . . The apples were very red on one side, and one was a beautiful green. It was a lovely little picture. Oh, what a fool I was! I think he would probably have let me have it. Anyhow, he came up to me and said quite quietly, 'You like that?' He spoke with a very strong accent, he smelt very strongly of garlic. I don't think he was very clean in his person. But of course, I was young and I didn't care a damn about that, and I said, 'Yes, master, I like that.' And then he did say – and this I know he said – 'It is very difficult to make apples round' . . . I began to say a long complicated sentence of how the English apples were round, the French apples were very inferior, were polyhedral. I got as far as 'polyhedral' and that started the dear old man off about spheres – he talked about cones and spheres, and I was rather bored, and I went on looking at the picture and he sort of faded away . . . What a wonderful story I could tell if he had expressed himself in a most amazing manner, and I could have quoted him . . .

Within a year he was dead, and I have for fifty years lost no opportunity of seeing every Cézanne picture that was being shown.

* Towards the end of his life Cézanne made several large paintings of the nude in landscape, including one of women bathers which is in the National Gallery, London. These pictures influenced Picasso – an artist whom Kelly admitted he did not understand, and whom he described as a 'subjectival' painter, while seeing himself as 'objectival'.

He has been a great tease to me. If only I had liked them all, or disliked them all, it would have been better, but every now and then I saw things which were lovely, wonderful, and then I saw acres of canvas that other people were admiring, where I could see just nothing. He was a giant, and for me, alas, he was a giant who didn't come off . . . Why is it that so much of Cézanne is no good to me at all? Very odd, and very annoying. . . .

Gerald Kelly as a young man in the 1890s.

Windsor Castle, a watercolour, April 1897 (8" × 11½").

The Vicar in his Study, portrait of Kelly's
father, 1912 (oil, 46″ × 37½″).

CHAPTER THREE

The 'Chat Blanc'

I

MEN AND THE WORLD (From Our Correspondent)
London, Saturday – Mr Gerald Kelly, the young British painter, whose work has attracted so much attention in Parisian art circles, and whose latest Salon picture was bought by the French Government for the Luxembourg, will be represented at the forthcoming Irish Exhibition at the Guildhall by his 'Monelle', a study of the heroine of Marcel Schwob's story. Mr Kelly, who is the only son of the Rev. F. F. Kelly, the well-known Vicar of Camberwell, is an Old Etonian and a Cambridge graduate, and did not begin painting till he went down from the 'Varsity. Though he did not enter any of the Paris studios, but studied independently, he met with immediate success, his first two pictures being hung on the line at the Salon of 1902.

The Irish Times, 23 May 1904

The above paragraph summarizes Kelly's achievement after two or three years in Paris. His success surprised no one more than himself. From the beginning he concentrated on portrait-painting, with landscape as a side-line. The first two pictures he sent to the Salon, which were hung on the line, were both portraits of his sister Rose – he only submitted them reluctantly on the urgent prompting of a friend.

A year or so later, after a picture of his had been bought in 1903 by the French Government, Kelly was having a glass of beer in a café when he overheard some students at the next table talking about him and his work. They were not complimentary, and concluded with the indictment: 'The fellow cannot draw a hand.'

Kelly thought about this, and next day consulted a French doctor, who gave him a lesson in bone construction. At the Louvre, he began to copy hands in pictures by Titian and Rembrandt. When drinking at a café, he would put down his left hand and make a drawing of it. He drew the hands of Marguerite Moréno, the actress-wife of his friend Marcel Schwob, the Jewish essayist and critic (who died young in 1905). Through her, he met Sarah Bernhardt, and he drew her hands in her dressing-room, while she recited a poem by Victor Hugo.

Kelly owed many glowing Parisian memories to the Schwobs; he would have painted Madame Schwob's portrait if it had not been for her husband's untimely death. The Schwobs were concerned for his welfare. Marguerite was worried because his French was too poor for him to understand the plays he heard on the stage. One day Marcel Schwob told him: 'You must break yourself of using certain vulgar words and phrases that you have picked up. There is a young man of immense promise who is hideously poor and very proud. I will arrange that you two should dine together once or even twice a week. You will pay for the dinner, and he will wean you from these vulgarisms.'

The young man was Paul Léautaud (1872–1956), best known for his absorbing literary diary. He was, like Kelly, a beautiful reader of verse. Kelly soon began a portrait of him. Léautaud writes: 'He did an amazing sketch of me, full of promise, in fact I could almost say admirable. It's full of simplicity and truth.' (13 November 1903.) This little low-toned oil-painted panel was never advanced to a finished portrait; it remains a memorial to Kelly's youthful impressionism, which had in it a touch of genius. After the sitting, they went to the Gaîté Montparnasse. They talked of Degas; and Léautaud was so taken by the music-hall that he told Kelly that, if he had been a painter, he would 'never have ventured further than portraits and music-hall scenes'. They became good friends. More than thirty years later, Léautaud, re-arranging his furniture, remembered 'le fauteuil anglais que m'a donné Kelley, au temps que je le voyais chez Schwob.' (16 June 1937.) Writing to James Harding, near the end of his life, Kelly confessed: 'I was very fond of Léautaud, and I never knew why. I thought him a great man. He was a wonderful talker, and I don't think what he wrote down gave us a fair sight of him.' (14 April 1970.)

Through Schwob, Kelly met a young man called Enoch Arnold Bennett. It was as 'Enoch' that Kelly knew him ('such a lovely name'). Kelly and Bennett were given tickets to see Eleanora Duse in a Russian play; Kelly was deeply impressed, but, when cross-examined by Marguerite Moréno, had to admit he had not the least idea what the play was about, and nor had Bennett. He was given such a severe dressing-down that he was reduced to tears.

In this way Kelly's social education proceeded, and he must have made progress, for in 1904 Clive Bell found him speaking French 'fluently and correctly'. Arnold Bennett also benefited. The latter, twelve years older than Kelly, was still a somewhat awkward, uncouth figure, overbearing but ill at ease in Bohemian society. Two entries from his diary confirm this:

> 22 June 1904 . . . I came across Kelly and others at the Café de Versailles, and stayed talking some time. The evening outdoor life of Montparnasse, in its circles so exclusively English and American, makes no appeal to me at all. . . .
>
> 27 June 1904 . . . I went down to Kelly's studio, a very large one, and he showed me a lot of his work which interested me very much. He made some good remarks about the present condition of painting. He said painters were afraid of making mistakes, afraid of being vulgar, and that they never used their eyes in search of material. They all painted the same things. He said some artist had said to him: 'We paint like governesses.' I certainly thought Kelly was doing good and original work, both in landscape and portraiture. Afterwards he took me to dine at the 'Chat Blanc'. Stanlaws, the 'creator' of the 'Stanlaws girl', was there, a terrible American, and also a girl I had previously seen at Kelly's. The girl and Stanlaws and the man who was the girl's host threw bread at each other, and sang American songs very loudly. It was terrible at times. . . .

The group to which Kelly belonged frequented an upper room at the 'Chat Blanc' in the Rue d'Odessa. Both Clive Bell and Somerset Maugham have described its habitués. Rodin appeared occasionally, and two of the more interesting painters were James Wilson Morrice, the Canadian, and the formidable Roderick O'Conor. Clive Bell says that Kelly was his closest friend during the summer of 1904 – 'a man of wit, culture, and ideas, far better educated and more alert than the majority of his companions in the quarter'. Kelly was glad to have the friendship of this brilliant young enthusiast, with whom he could discuss literature as well as art. But J. W. Morrice was a man of gusto who influenced Kelly as an artist (both also being affected, at this time, by Whistler).

Another influence on Kelly was John Singer Sargent. Kelly wrote to Charles Mount, Sargent's biographer (29 June 1954): 'He was outrageously kind to me, who could give nothing in return. He was one of the most shy, modest creatures I have ever met.'

No one did more for Kelly as a young artist, however, than Sir Hugh Lane, the Irish art collector, dealer, and critic, who went down with the *Lusitania* in 1915, when he was only forty. Lane had great charm; a dandy and a gambler, fastidious but sociable. He acquired in Paris many of the works he collected for his Dublin gallery of modern art, opened in 1908, in which Kelly was well represented by 'Mrs Harrison' and 'At the Stage Door', both painted in Paris in 1906–7. It was Sarah Purser who first saw a picture of Kelly's in Paris and advised Lane to buy it. 'He became my earliest and greatest patron,' Kelly told an *Irish Times* interviewer in 1950: 'All my first twenty commissions – and those are the ones that count! – I got through Lane.' Kelly painted a fine three-quarter-length portrait of Lane, which once belonged to Lane's sister.

Hugh Lane formed a collection of modern pictures for the municipal gallery at Johannesburg. Lady Gregory, in her book on him, says that when she saw a photograph of the opening in 1910, in which Lane is shown talking earnestly to the Duke of Connaught, she remarked: 'I am sure Hugh is advising the Duke to have his portrait painted by Kelly.' A pertinent comment, for a Kelly portrait of Lady Gregory was to appear in the 1914 Academy.

2

A disturbing figure in the circle at the 'Chat Blanc' was the eccentric magician, Aleister Crowley, who, since his Cambridge acquaintance with Kelly, had been climbing mountains with Oscar Eckenstein (1859–1921) in Mexico and the Himalayas. The pair had kept in touch by letter, and Crowley now came to stay with Kelly at his studio in Montparnasse. Crowley was introduced to Marcel Schwob, Rodin, and Arnold Bennett; he includes an account of his life in Paris in his unreliable *Confessions*. Somerset Maugham knew him too, and said he 'took an immediate dislike to him'; but he added: 'he interested and amused me . . . He was a fake, but not entirely a fake.'

Francis Toye, in his autobiography, shows Crowley as a practical joker of a certain engaging quality. With his remaining wealth, he acquired an estate called Boleskine on Loch Ness, and it was there, reported Toye, that 'he is said to have invited a certain Swiss gentleman "to come and hunt the haggis" . . . One summer evening, just as they were about to sit down to dinner, a servant, primed of course beforehand, ran into the room and, dropping on one knee, exclaimed: "My lord, my lord! The haggis is on the hill!" Crowley and the unsus-

pecting Swiss snatched their guns and rushed out. It was beginning to
get dark, but there was still light enough to distinguish not far away an
animal with a a pair of horns. (It was in fact an elderly ram procured for
the occasion.) The Swiss fired both his barrels; there were yells of
delight from the "retainers", and the proud visitor was about to run
forward to claim his victim when Crowley stopped him with a warning
that according to local tradition the haggis must never be approached
by him who has killed it; presently the carcass would be brought in
state to the hall. So the two returned to their dinner, and sure enough,
later there entered a small procession led by a piper, carrying the now
skinned animal. Then, after several perambulations, the horns were
ceremoniously presented to the Swiss, who, they say, took them back
to Switzerland and affixed them, duly labelled and dated, to the walls
of his villa. . . .'

The equally bizarre but much more tragic story of Crowley's
involvement with the Kelly family must now be told. In July 1903,
Kelly visited Crowley at Boleskine, while his mother went for a cure
to nearby Strathpeffer, accompanied by her widowed daughter Rose.
Kelly and Crowley travelled over to stay with them, Crowley wearing
Highland dress. Rose asked her brother's advice in a personal dilemma;
being an inveterate flirt, she had become involved with South African
and American suitors, both of whom she had rashly promised to marry.
Crowley suggested as a quixotic solution a platonic marriage with
himself, and soon they were secretly married by a lawyer at Dingwall
at eight o'clock in the morning.

The above paragraph is based on the biography of Crowley by John
Symonds. Crowley's account in his *Confessions* adds other details. He
mentions that Kelly's mother 'worthily preserved the conditions of
Tennysonian dignity', and that Rose 'was in a curious state of excitement'. He says he made his strange proposal to Rose on the links at
Strathpeffer, while Kelly was playing a round of golf. And after describing the marriage at Dingwall he adds:

> Gerald Kelly burst into the room, his pale face drawn with
> insane passion . . . On learning that we were already married, he
> aimed a violent blow at me. It missed me by about a yard. I am
> ashamed to say that I could not repress a quiet smile. If he had not
> been out of his mind, his action would have been truly courageous,
> for compared with me he was a shrimp. . . .

Whatever their original intentions may have been, it became clear
that Rose had fallen passionately in love with her dubious saviour, and

that Crowley was equally infatuated with her. They went on a pro-longed honeymoon, travelling to Ceylon, and for some time lived happily together. By March 1904, when they were in Cairo, their passion had subsided; Crowley received some magical revelation, and began to call himself Prince Chioa Khan – a title which he insisted Mrs Kelly should use in addressing letters to her daughter.

The Kellys were now viewing Crowley with consternation which eventually grew to alarm. But Rose was expecting a child, and Gerald and his friend Ivor Back, the surgeon, both stayed at Boleskine in 1904 during her confinement. A daughter was born, who died in 1906. A second daughter, Lola, born in 1907, survived into adulthood. Crowley still had a chance, as his biographer John Symonds put it, 'of settling down and getting on with the business of ordinary living'; apparently 'he kicked his mother-in-law downstairs instead'.

In 1909 the Crowleys were divorced. Rose was married once again, to a Dr Goymley. She died in 1932, while Aleister Crowley lived on, thoroughly disgraced, until 1947.

Rose was a charming, attractive, if somewhat scatterbrained woman, who paid dearly for any frivolity in her behaviour. Gerald Kelly had always been fond of his sister; her humiliation left him with a lasting hatred for Crowley, and a sense of disillusionment that sharpened his distrust of every *poseur* he later encountered.

John Napper, who was Kelly's assistant in the late nineteen-thirties, remembers a maid coming into the studio to announce that 'a Mr Crowley was at the front door. G. K. threw down his brushes and rushed off down the passage. There was the sound of a violent alterca-tion and a shriek, the front door slammed and G. K. came back into the studio looking exactly like a bantam cock – and in such a rage that he could hardly speak for five minutes.'

Somerset Maugham published a novel *The Magician* (1908), in which Crowley served as a model for the principal character Oliver Haddo, though Maugham emphasized in a later introduction that he had made his character 'more sinister and more ruthless than Crowley ever was'. Rose's plight may well have suggested the thraldom of Haddo's wife Margaret. Crowley read *The Magician* and attributed the details of his own life and Maugham's knowledge of magic to Gerald Kelly, whom Crowley had introduced in 1899 to an esoteric occult society, the Hermetic Order of the Golden Dawn. Kelly's membership of the society was brief, but Crowley's diagnosis was probably correct. Kelly had become a close friend of Maugham. Indeed, their friendship was so important to both men that it deserves a new chapter.

CHAPTER FOUR

Maugham's Friend

I

William Somerset Maugham was, in a peculiar way, Anglo-French from birth, for he was born in the British Embassy in Paris in 1874. Legal and literary influences in his family help to explain why one of his brothers, Frederic, was Lord Chancellor, and why he himself was a novelist. His elder brother Charles became a solicitor, and partner in the Paris firm of 'Maugham et Dixon, jurisconsultes anglais', which had been founded by their father, Robert Ormond Maugham. As the father was solicitor to the British Embassy, it had been easy to arrange for his son to be born on what was technically British soil, and thus escape the obligation of serving in the French forces.

Somerset Maugham spent his childhood in Paris, until, at the age of ten, on the death of his parents, he was taken to live with an uncle in England and sent to school at Canterbury. Between his leaving the school in 1890 and his meeting with Kelly at his brother Charles's villa in 1903, Maugham obtained a great deal of experience; he travelled over much of Europe, qualified as a doctor, and wrote *Liza of Lambeth*.

Maugham and Kelly were cosmopolitan by instinct. Both had been idle at school. Both were candid, intelligent, artistic (Kelly introduced Maugham to the Impressionists). Even where they differed, it was to the advantage of their friendship. Kelly was a great talker; Maugham, because of his stammer, was not. 'While I have leaned on his patience and on his wisdom, he has often been exasperated by my verbosity,' wrote Kelly in a tribute on Maugham's eightieth birthday in *The Sunday Times* (24 January 1954); and he added, 'I am a great chatterbox and he is a reflective, silent man.' The same source gives Kelly's account of their meeting in the autumn of 1903, when he was twenty-four and Maugham twenty-nine:

I first met Somerset Maugham in the garden of a villa which his elder brother had taken for the summer at Meudon. I was struck by the fact that his whole face was just one colour – very pale – and that his eyes were like little pieces of brown velvet – like monkey's eyes. I thought he looked very distinguished.

It was not strange that we became friends. We accepted each other for what we believed ourselves to be – he a promising young writer and I a promising young painter. . . .

We had in common also that both of us obstinately refused to pretend to admire what really we did not admire – even when we had been told we should admire it. Willie dared to find Meredith and Pater overrated; I was bold enough to love Ingres and Manet – unfashionable judgements at the beginning of this century. I am sure that Willie has never departed from that kind of integrity; and in my own way I, too, have tried never to become a sycophant or a hypocrite.

It might be added that Kelly and Maugham were both small men with hot tempers. Kelly's features had settled into a characteristically Irish, independent face; he was probably wearing a Lavallière bow, which Clive Bell imitated. Kelly's relatively undisciplined life was to excite Maugham's criticism.

The earliest surviving letters from Maugham to Kelly (undated but probably of 1904) were written from the Bath Club, Dover Street, and from a flat near Victoria Station he was sharing with his friend Walter Payne. They set the tone for many that followed during the next sixty years – namely, a lively practical interest in Kelly's work and a consistent wish to advise, admonish, and encourage him in his career. In these first letters, he inquires Kelly's fee for a portrait of his sister-in-law, and says he is trying to get him a commission to do a poster for one of his plays.

While he was still in London, Maugham asked Kelly to find him an apartment in Montparnasse. Kelly discovered one near the Lion de Belfort, not far from his own studio; the address was 3 Rue Victor Considérant. Maugham moved in at the end of February 1905. While Kelly was away in April, travelling for his health, Maugham looked after his studio and tried to pay his bills (including 114 francs to the 'Chat Blanc') from the sum allowed to him, but found he had to apply for help to Camberwell Vicarage. Maugham proposed they should share his *femme de ménage*; as Kelly got up later than he did, she could come to him (Maugham) first.

Arnold Bennett was becoming a social challenge for Maugham, as he had already become for Kelly. In April 1905, Maugham told Kelly that he was beginning to like Bennett, but that it was painful to be with him. Kelly elaborated on this in the article in *The Sunday Times* already quoted:

> Bennett was really rather a preposterous person; his appearance was outrageous and his manners uncouth. He was, besides, terribly bumptious, very conscious of deficiencies in his education, and therefore rather offensively self-defensive. But I liked him, and used to dine with him once a month. One evening we were dining together in a cheap restaurant in Montparnasse,* and I introduced him and Willie – who was also eating there – to each other. Willie was his exact opposite in everything – dapper, neat, cultivated, and urbane – and they disliked each other instinctively.
>
> During the evening Willie – with his impeccable French accent – said to the waitress: '*Vous me donnerez un anneau*,' meaning that he wanted a napkin ring so that he could reserve his napkin for the next time he dined there. 'You know, Maugham,' observed Bennett heavily, 'the French don't call it an "anno", they call it a "rong".' (He meant a *rond*.) Willie became quite grey with rage; to have made this absurd mistake and thus laid himself open to correction by a quite unspeakable individual whose knowledge of French was rudimentary! Yet – and this is the point of my story – some time later, when I returned from a trip to Burma and met Willie again, the first thing he said to me was: 'Gerald, Enoch Arnold has written a masterpiece.' And eventually his admiration for Bennett's lovely work – he was referring, of course, to *The Old Wives' Tale* – led to their becoming firm friends.

Soon Bennett was noting in his diary: 'Maugham, Kelly and I dined together *chez* Liseux last night. They came in here afterwards, the two of them, and I enjoyed them.' (7 October 1905.)

Maugham's letters make it clear that 1905 was a disturbed year for Kelly. He wrote to him severely from Capri on 24 July:

> . . . I am very sorry, though by no means surprised, that you have fallen ill again. It is obvious to the meanest intelligence that if you lead such a life as you led in Paris you are quite sure to be ill. A much stronger constitution than yours would go to pieces if such tricks were played with it as you play. You often ate nothing at

* Probably the 'Chat Blanc'.

all till one or two & then again not till nine or after; you took no exercise & never went in the fresh air. I am willing to bet a comparatively large sum that within a month of your return to Paris you will be just as bad as ever. I cannot write to you with any patience. By the stupidest carelessness (and I daresay at the bottom of your heart the feeling that it's very romantic & pictur-esque to cultivate a fine frenzy which ignores the matter of fact) you are throwing away all your chances of becoming a better painter than Tom, Dick, or Harry. For the work you do when you're not well is rotten & you know as well as I do that no one has ever done valuable stuff unless he was backed by a vigorous physique. Do not take this lecture in bad part, but devise means whereby you may work well & keep healthy . . .

In the autumn of 1905, Maugham had to lecture Kelly again – this time for having decided to throw in his lot with a young dancer and live with her in Montmartre. Maugham saw it was useless to argue the question, though he thought the move would harm Kelly's work, but he warned him that the new ménage would be expensive, and rejoiced that he himself was not passionately involved with anyone. Paul Léautaud, in his diary of 20 November 1906, confirmed that Kelly and his dancer were living in the Rue Tourlaque behind the Montmartre cemetery. He plied Kelly with compliments in the hope of making him get on with his portrait. But he wrote as if disillusioned: 'Boaster and fop, as he is, he was delighted. He who used to be clean-shaven in the English fashion has grown a moustache. The power of love!' The moustache proved as temporary as the liaison. Ironically, Maugham himself became seriously involved in 1906 with an English actress, Ethelwyn Sylvia Jones, daughter of the dramatist Henry Arthur Jones and destined to be the original of the promiscuous Rosie in *Cakes and Ale*. Kelly also admired 'Sue', as she was called, and painted her por-trait, which Maugham described in the book as the work of 'Lionel Hillier'.

2

Having become a member of the Salon d'Automne in 1904, Kelly soon looked for opportunities to exhibit in London, at the Grafton Galleries, Grosvenor Gallery, and other places. He was a founder-member of the Modern Portrait Painters Society in 1907, and of the National Portrait

Society in 1910, and became an Associate of the Royal Hibernian
Academy in 1908. He first exhibited at the Royal Academy in 1909.

Maugham abandoned his Paris apartment after 1905, but during his
frequent travels he kept up his correspondence with Kelly, and he
visited the London exhibitions at which his friend was represented,
constantly encouraging him and analysing his contributions in detail.
Kelly made two portraits of Maugham in 1907 (of which one was
destroyed); they were the first of eighteen portraits he painted of him.
In September of that year Maugham, who had previously always written
'My dear Kelly', began a letter 'My dear Rembrandt'. Having broken
through the conventions, he opened in future with 'My dear Gerald'.

In March 1908, while Maugham was at the outset of his great success
as a dramatist, and was rehearsing his play *Jack Straw*, he wrote con-
doling with Kelly on the ending of his romantic 'idyll' – which had
not come as a surprise to him. Kelly was greatly upset, however:

> I must have been desperately much in love, for how desperately
> unhappy I was when she left me for another. I didn't care for
> anything; I even stopped painting.
>
> Then a friend – actually, Mr Somerset Maugham – advised me to
> take a nice long journey which would help me to forget her
> (though, of course, I knew I never would).
>
> I had seen some snapshots of Burmese dancers, and so, with the
> sublime spontaneous stupidity of youth, I just went off to Burma.
> How lucky, how wonderfully lucky, I was. (Preface to catalogue
> of exhibition of his Burmese paintings, 1962.)

He found himself on the same ship, on the long voyage in the summer
of 1908, as an Old Etonian who had been appointed District Judge in
Mandalay, and for six months he was able to make the judge's home his
headquarters, while he travelled up and down the Irrawaddy by steamer
and rode inland by pony. Of Mandalay he wrote:

> Try and imagine how beautiful it was. A square mile surrounded
> by high, rosy brick walls and sunrise and sunset all over it. And
> how sweet the women and children were.
>
> So many pretty ones. Alas, I had no Burmese, so I could not tell
> the charming young ladies there that I had forgotten the girl in
> Paris.

The visit to Burma – generously supported by Maugham with a draft
of £50 on a Rangoon bank – gave Kelly's art a new dimension. He
worked continually in the last months of 1908 and early months of

1909, painting small landscapes and studies of Burmese girls, many of
which were reassembled at his retrospective Royal Academy exhibition
of 1957. One of his most ambitious compositions was called 'Yein
Pwé: Pagan', and was based on a study of dancers painted at Pagan in
1909. But the Burmese picture most likely to be remembered is one of
the dancer Ma Si Gyaw (Plate 6) begun at Mandalay in 1909 and presented by Francis Howard to the Tate Gallery in 1914. Kelly painted
her about 36 times.

Another model was the dancer Ma Seyn Mé, of whom he made
numerous sketches over a period of three months. Some he completed
in oils; others he eventually enlarged to life-size pictures, though they
mostly remained unfinished. 'Of course I didn't speak one word of
Burmese,' Kelly told Mrs Rotha Barnfield in 1940, 'but I had an
interpreter & Ma Seyn Mé was so gay & full of zestful life that we had
very lively sittings. I used to go – rather a gate-crasher – to any dance
where she was performing.'

The delicacy and neatness of these girls, and the colours of their
clothes, suited the precision and high finish of Kelly's craftmanship as
it developed after the First World War. The public liked them, and
some became familiar in popular prints. His pre-occupation received a
fresh impetus in 1931 when his friend Sir Harcourt Butler, knowing he
appreciated pretty Burmese girls, invited him to lunch and put him
next to Saw Ohn Nyun, sister-in-law of the Rajah of Thi-Paw. She had
come to England to learn English, and was joined by her sister and her
husband who was attending a conference. Kelly described their meeting:

> She was very pretty and bored to tears. Her sister went to formal
> parties and she was not invited, and as she had nothing whatever
> to do I coaxed her into sitting for me. She sat for about two months
> almost every day. I did as much as I could, I wished I had done
> more . . . I began about eight pictures which I have been playing
> with ever since. (Letter to Captain W. B. Houston, 1961.)

Some of these pictures were among Kelly's most successful in this
genre. A visit to Cambodia in 1937 provided him with further material,
so that he was able to maintain his output of charming eastern ladies
until the end of his life; indeed one of them appeared at the Academy
in the summer exhibition after his death. He had rolls of silk for their
dresses stored in his studio (and none was ever allowed to be folded).

3

While he was in Paris, Kelly began his career as a versatile collector of works of art, furniture, and objects of all kinds. He became a busy magpie who in time filled his London home with treasures, including many bottles of wine. If he had a starting-point, perhaps it was the Gillot sale of Japanese prints and books in Paris in 1904. He attended this auction with his mother, acquiring one of a famous series of mica-background prints of courtesans by Eishi. His mother held the purse-strings; he was annoyed that she did not allow him to bid for another print.

In Paris he also obtained a trunk-full of Second Empire wall-papers which he thought he might use to decorate his studio. He never did; at the end of his life he presented them to the Victoria and Albert Museum.

Another passion dating from the nineties was for Aubrey Beardsley, of whom Kelly became a distinguished collector. Several of the best drawings in the famous 1966 Beardsley exhibition at the V. and A. had once been in his hands; some of these are now in the V. and A. Print Room. Brian Reade, who organized the exhibition, asked Kelly whether he had met Beardsley. 'No,' replied Kelly, 'I was once at a party in the nineties when Beardsley was present surrounded by admirers, but he was too grand and I was too shy, so I never spoke to him.'

4

Kelly stayed in Burma much longer than Somerset Maugham thought prudent. He told Kelly in a letter postmarked 1 March 1909 that Hugh Lane had five portraits for him to paint, but that Lane could not induce these potential clients to wait indefinitely for his return. He warned him that Lane might lose interest, and reminded him that portrait painting was his chief strength; his pictures at the recent Modern Portrait Painters' exhibition had not attracted so much attention as last year's, he said, while Orpen and Nicholson – whom Maugham considered Kelly's chief rivals – had advanced their reputations. Maugham urged him not to be self-willed and fitful, and ended with what he called 'a moral exhortation':

. . . Many people have just as much talent as you & it does not avail them for want of character, & I know many people who have infinitely more strength of character than you, but that too does not avail them because they lack the talent: genius is a combination of talent and character, but character to a certain extent – I do not know how much, but I believe enormously – can be acquired: but you cannot acquire it without a certain effort. You seem to me to have hereditarily more against you than most people, but that does not matter if you only see the facts clearly & arm yourself against them. . . .

Maugham was relieved to know, when he next wrote on 17 April 1909, that Kelly was on his way back to Europe. And, after his traumatic experience, it was to London, not Paris, that he returned. Maugham begged him to acquire a studio in the west end, promising to advance the money if his father would not do so; he felt it was amateurish to go on painting people in a Camberwell vicarage. That Kelly responded to this plea is suggested by the fact that his three Academy portraits of 1910 were submitted from 6 William Street, Lowndes Square. But we know that at least one of these was painted in Camberwell, because the sitter Elizabeth Heygate (Plate 5b) wrote a vivid account of the experience in her book *A Girl at Eton*.

Elizabeth was the teenage daughter of an Eton housemaster, A. C. G. Heygate; Kelly had written to Heygate offering to paint a member of his family 'for a low fee', and Elizabeth had been chosen. She travelled by train to Waterloo with her mother, and they carried a cardboard box containing three dresses: pink silk (favoured by Elizabeth), white organdie, and 'an old accordion-pleated dress that had been dyed black' for a funeral (which Elizabeth did not like at all). Kelly was to be invited to choose.

> . . . We took a taxi [wrote Elizabeth], swerving past lines of clanging trams, to a vicarage in Camberwell, where Mr Kelly lived with his father. Initial shyness gave way to curiosity and surprise as we followed the parlourmaid down a passage and she knocked on the drawing-room door. It burst open and a small dark man appeared. Talking volubly to Mother, he paid no attention to me, so I walked to the French windows opening on to a large garden, which seemed strangely remote from the rows of sordid houses and noisy streets outside.
>
> Mother undid the cardboard box and shook out the dresses . . . while I prayed for Mr Kelly's taste to coincide with mine. He filled a pipe and stared at the creased garments.
>
> 'Put on the black one,' he said abruptly, and I knew that I was

doomed to suffer in future, portrayed for all to see in deepest mourning.

I undressed behind a screen, adding black shoes and stockings to this melancholy outfit . . .

Kelly circled round 'like an energetic beetle' and gave Elizabeth a peacock's feather to hold. When her mother objected that this was unlucky, he said: 'Superstitions are damn rot . . . And now undo that pigtail and shake out your hair.' Elizabeth continued her description:

Sheltered at Eton from risky subjects and bad language, my first acquaintance with a Bohemian world was stimulating, and drew me to this strange Old Etonian in fearful expectation. The Beetle swore without apology, making Mother wince. He discussed the love-affairs of a ballet-dancer who had sat for him while Mother listened with averted eyes. Father had paid for the picture in advance and, in spite of his distressing manners, Mother hoped that he might land the family with a masterpiece. Absorbed in painting, the Beetle forgot my stiffening limbs and when I began to fidget he compared me unfavourably with other sitters. . . .

'That's all,' he said one afternoon, throwing his palette on a table.

Mother got up and stared at the wet paint.

'It is an excellent likeness,' she said.

'Likeness be damned. The girl's face is of little importance; look at those bones,' he leant forward following the line of my arms and legs with the stem of his pipe. 'Very fine and the devil to paint.'

Delighted by any praise, I stood in front of the picture, concentrating on a face I scarcely recognized. My hair, loosened from the restraining pigtail, stood out full of unexpected lights, making a warm background for my pale face. The eyes accentuated by thick arched brows looked larger than my own, and I realized with a stab of pleasure that Mr Kelly had found the lively spirit lying beneath my lack of beauty, and had given my face a hitherto unknown distinction.

5

Kelly now considered himself officially domiciled in London, and through the efforts of Maugham and his friend Walter Payne he was elected a member of the Bath Club. Maugham's letters to Kelly at this time (1910–11) reflect their mutual interest in the work of James Pryde, whose robust romantic theatrical canvases appealed to them both; Kelly had advised Pryde to paint on a smaller scale, and in 1911 Pryde was trying to sell Maugham a little picture for £175, which Maugham thought too much.

But Kelly, like Maugham, was too restless to stay in London for many months on end. Early in 1911, with Maugham's encouragement, he went to Seville in search of fresh inspiration; and he spent most of the next few years painting in Spain. Maugham contrasted his Burmese and Spanish achievements in an article:

> . . . His Burmese dancers . . . have a strange impenetrability, their gestures are enigmatic and yet significant, they are charming, and yet there is something curiously hieratic in their manner; with a sure instinct, and with a more definite feeling for decoration than is possible in a portrait, Mr Kelly has given us the character of the East as we of our generation see it. It needed a peculiar sensitiveness; and the same sensitiveness has served him in painting Andalusia. Here again it is the character of a race that he has painted, more intimately than when he painted the Burmese, because the soul of the Spaniard is nearer to us than that of the Oriental, and here again he has shown a rare originality . . . He has painted Andalusia . . . with fresh eyes and from an entirely personal standpoint; and they who know the country must realize the truth of his presentment. For Andalusia is a land of passion, and passion is not mirthful, there is always tragedy at the back of the dancing and the laughter which are all the superficial see; and the songs of its people are a melancholy wailing: they deal with unrequited love and death and hunger. *Rosa Maria* and the woman of *The Black Shawl*, with her beautifully painted hand, have eyes heavy with tears, their faces are sensual with a sensuality raised to a strange height of passion. There is the real Andalusia, and the painter who could see it, breaking through a shallow tradition, has gifts of insight which are rare among his fellows. ('A Student of Character', *International Studio*, December 1914.)

If Kelly's Burmese dancers were painted with a certain Anglo-Saxon detachment, his shawled Spanish beauties attested an essential Irishness, and an innate partiality for Spain. And sometimes, as in 'The Basket-makers', there was an open tribute to Velasquez. Another result of his new enthusiasm, was a collector's interest in Spanish wood-carvings. He also learned to speak Spanish well.

During these pre-war years, Kelly alternated between long stays in Spain and portrait-painting in London. It was in his studio at 7 William Street, in the summer of 1911, that Maugham gave him thirty to forty sittings for 'The Jester' (Plate 7), which was eventually bought for the Tate Gallery under the Chantrey Bequest. The portrait was one of the most attractive and spontaneous Kelly ever painted, capturing with a touch of affectionate mockery a morning call from the fashionable playwright at the height of his career. Another subsequent Chantrey purchase was Kelly's portrait of his own father (Plate 2) painted in the following year; Pryde as well as Whistler may have influenced him here.

Maugham was a faithful correspondent, concerned and anxious for his friend's success, always ready to offer a loan of money in difficult times. As a letter-writer Kelly was less predictable. Maugham sent him a postcard to Seville in September 1913, with the single word 'WRITE' in the centre and the words 'Do it Now' repeated at each of the four corners.

By the summer of 1914, Kelly had established himself as a leading portrait-painter. Writing to Seville in May, Maugham was able to tell him that he had three pictures in the Academy exhibition, two of them on the line; that they had received good notices in the *Mail* and *The Observer*, and that *The Times* had called his portrait of Lady Gregory the best in the show.

In the autumn of 1914, Maugham was serving in Flanders with the Red Cross; this did not last long, and in January 1915, he was staying in Rome with Mrs Syrie Wellcome, whom he married after a divorce. He then spent a year in Switzerland working for British Intelligence, and in 1917 travelled to Russia as a chief agent. He had an interview with Kerensky, who gave him a message for Lloyd George, but the October Revolution of 1917 put an end to Maugham's Russian activities.

Meanwhile Kelly became exhausted in transferring his parents and himself, after his father's retirement from Camberwell in 1915, to the tall Georgian house at 65 (later 117) Gloucester Place, Portman Square, where he was to live and work (he built a large studio in the garden) for the next fifty years and more. Kelly described the circumstances of his father's retirement to Mr. C. Jennings:

> . . . I hope I am right in thinking that my father was a competent Vicar of Camberwell: but he did not 'suffer fools gladly' and he was impatient with anything that smacked of humbug. He called himself, and he was, a Tory of Tories, and he had advanced views

about social welfare . . . Among the local clergy the Herberts of
Vauxhall, Mr Dyke (Vicar of Dulwich I think and Rural Dean) and
your father were the ones that he respected.

My father suffered terribly from neuritis and became very
lame. He stuck the pain bravely, but it was slowly brought home
to him that he ought to resign. My grandfather had bought him the
advowson of Camberwell and the value of this had been taken
into consideration in my grandfather's will. Though my father
thought it wrong that advowsons should be private property, and
he would have liked to present it to the Diocese, he felt he ought
to get *some* thing for it for my sake.

While he was hesitating, Dr Burge, newly consecrated Bishop
of Southwark, came and told my father he must go. A more
patient approach would have given that 'proud prelate' the chance
of recognizing that old Mr Kelly was not so bad as he thought. My
father was too disgusted to explain, but he asked your father to
represent him in the negotiations that followed. Mother and I
were delighted and touched by 'dear old Jennings' ' amazing skill
and charm and patience between his Bishop, whom he had to
respect, and my father who had his naughty moments.

(Letter, 12 February 1949, to Mr C. Jennings, son of Rev. H. E.
Jennings, Vicar of St Clements, Dulwich, whose portrait Kelly painted
in 1916.)

His father died in 1918, aged 80, in the house in Gloucester Place;
but before then Kelly had, like Maugham, involved himself – no doubt
on Maugham's recommendation – as an intelligence agent in Spain.
Evidence of what he actually accomplished there is tantalizingly slight,
but some idea of it can be gained from Maugham's book of spy stories,
Ashenden. This was dedicated to Kelly, who said:

'He and I were in the intelligence department during the war.
He was in Switzerland and Russia. I was in Spain. The book is a
composite one of our experiences. I furnished him with three of
the seven episodes. Do you remember the story of "The Hairless
Mexican"? That happened to me. Only the true story is better
than you find it in the book. There the wrong man was killed.
Actually we trailed him, spent £100 of good allied money following him. Watched him go to the station at Seville, get into a
carriage bound for Madrid – and the rascal then slipped out the
other side and disappeared. (Diary of Dr F. W. Hilles, 24
November 1930.)

In another of the Ashenden stories, 'His Excellency', Maugham provided the most unequivocal of his many fictional portrayals of Kelly, whom he presented as the 'talented young Irish painter called O'Malley. He's an R. A. now and paints highly paid portraits of Lord Chancellors and Cabinet Ministers.' In the story Maugham's ambassador is made to continue:

> . . . He was good company, the type of the agreeable rattle, and he had a truly Irish gift of the gab. He talked incessantly and in my friend's opinion brilliantly. He found it very amusing to go and sit in the studio while O'Malley was painting and listen to him chattering away about the technique of his art.

It would be rash to assume that Kelly is rendered so completely in other Maugham characters, but there are many glimpses of him throughout Maugham's books. He served as a model for the aggressive Lawson in *Of Human Bondage*. When someone spoke disparagingly of Manet's 'Olympia', Lawson's 'green eyes flashed fire, he gasped with rage, but he could be seen imposing calm upon himself.' And further: 'Lawson had the pedagogic instinct; whenever he found anything out he was eager to impart it; and because he taught with delight he taught with profit.' Or again: 'A fine picture gave Lawson an immediate thrill. His appreciation was instinctive.'

It was natural that Maugham should turn to his memories of such an intimate friend when a painter had to be described. The result was often so transmuted that it could be misleading. Kelly said he was sure 'all Willie's bad painters are portraits of myself', but he only claimed to have given Maugham sound advice in one instance. He was asked to read the proofs of *The Moon and Sixpence*, Maugham's novel about Gauguin, published in 1919, and came to the passage in which the bad painter Stroeve was 'tempted to destroy the masterpiece which represented his own wife in the nude'.

> . . . I pointed out to Willie [he wrote in his *Sunday Times* article of 1954] that nobody could possibly slash a canvas with a palette knife – as he had described – since a palette knife bends and will not cut. With great erudition I suggested that he should indicate a 'scraper' instead, for a scraper is sharp and pointed. But he was unimpressed. No one, he said, would understand about a scraper whereas a palette knife sounded perfectly feasible. . . .

Maugham, nevertheless, substituted the word 'scraper'. He also presented Kelly with the manuscript of *The Moon and Sixpence*. It was perhaps a recognition of Kelly's influence on him at the time when they both became aware of Gauguin in Paris.

An undated wartime letter to Kelly from George Moore, probably of 1917, emphasizes that his literary judgement was valued by writers. It concerns Kelly's comment on a re-issue of Moore's early work *Lewis Seymour and Some Women*:

> . . . I love to be read by painters, for that they are the only critics of literature is a truth that I have always held by. When ever I hear anything to the point about a book the remark comes from a painter. It requires more talent to paint than to write, I think, indeed I am sure it does. . . .

6

The most important event of Kelly's war years was his meeting in 1916 with his future wife. She was Lilian, fifth daughter of the eight children of Simon Ryan. It was a working-class family, and Lilian sat as an artist's model under the selective guidance of Sir George Clausen, R.A., who advised her on which invitations she should accept. Fortunately for Kelly, Clausen allowed her to sit for him.

The meeting in 1916 did not seem significant at the time, as Kelly soon set off for Spain, and Lilian forgot all about him. But in 1919 he wrote to her again, and she sat for him. After she left, he went into another artist's studio and said: 'What a pity that girl's married!' The other artist was able to tell him he was mistaken.

The friendship then progressed, and in the Spring of 1920, while Lilian was sitting for Frank Cadogan Cowper, an extraordinary incident occurred. Cadogan Cowper, who stuttered, asked suddenly: 'Have you got a young man?' There was a very long silence, and he continued: 'You'll be married in three weeks' time.' Another silence. 'And I'll tell you who you are going to marry – Gerald Kelly.'

Considering that Cadogan Cowper did not know Kelly, this prediction suggests second sight, unless he had some private information. In fact, Lilian was much surprised when Kelly proposed. She was twenty-one; Gerald was twenty years older, though his vitality made him seem younger than his age. They were actually married at St Michael's, Paddington, on 15 April 1920, within fifteen days of Cadogan Cowper's prophecy, and went to Spain for the honeymoon (Plate 4).

Lilian brought to the marriage not only her beauty and charm but a quiet strength and sense of repose that Kelly badly needed to steady his restless energy. Henceforth his life received a new meaning and purpose. Maugham called the news of Kelly's marriage 'staggering', but thought he had done 'a very clever thing' and would 'make a great success of it, & be very happy'. So it proved; and Maugham became very fond of 'Jane'.

Kelly's wife lost both her surname and her Christian name, for she was always to be known by her husband's nickname of Jane. One of his many devoted and ingeniously varied portraits of Jane appeared at the Academy in 1921. His Diploma work on being elected R. A. in 1930 was to be 'Jane XXX' (Plate 8b; the Roman numerals in the titles of his portraits of Jane referred to the years of their first exhibition at the Academy). Jane's face became one of the best known in England.

The following Clerihew may have originated in a *New Statesman* competition:

> Mr Gerald Kelly
> Never paints Joan or Nelly –
> When at each show one sees Jane
> One can only gasp 'Again?'

And when later she was introduced to Queen Mary, Her Majesty exclaimed: 'Jane of the many Janes!'

CHAPTER FIVE

Fashionable Portrait-Painter

I

After her son's marriage, Kelly's mother moved to a new home. Gerald and Jane established themselves in Gloucester Place.

That they had no children was a disappointment for them. At one time, there were great hopes, but it was not to be. Later, they both came to feel that perhaps, for a man of Gerald's excitable temperament and intense artistic enthusiasm, fatherhood might have brought special complications.

The house, like Reynolds's in Leicester Square, became a portrait factory which grew increasingly busy as time went on. Many of the most distinguished men and women of the time passed through the front door, along the hall passage, and into the big studio. In its off-duty hours, the house was a centre of gracious, often lavish hospitality: a gathering-point for connoisseurs and artists. And, again like Sir Joshua, Kelly filled his rooms with pictures, books, miscellaneous art treasures; and his cellar with fine wines.

Kelly's earlier sitters, painted before 1914, had tended to be relatives, friends, or those, such as Elizabeth Heygate of Eton, who had some association with his personal life. Even the splendid portrait of old 'Mrs Harrison' (Plate 5a), which was bought by Sir Hugh Lane for Dublin in 1907 and may be said to have 'made his name', had a local association; for Mrs Harrison was the mother-in-law of his father's curate at Camberwell.

There was a warmth and humanity about much of this early work which Kelly rarely recaptured later. In terms of poetry and atmosphere, he never painted better than in those pre-war years which produced his Tate Gallery pictures 'The Jester' and 'The Vicar'. After the war he continued to respond artistically to actors and actresses like Doris

Lytton (1920) or Arthur Bourchier as Long John Silver (1924, Garrick Club), or to a striking character like Charles Whibley (1925–6, Jesus College, Cambridge). His conscientious craftsmanship and self-effacing detachment ensured a high level of achievement in any portrait he undertook. But he became to some extent a victim of his success. The long procession of the eminent who eventually sat to him made it necessary to save time by the use of photography. This may have tended to induce a certain flatness, a lack of spatial depth, which contrasted with the earlier work.

One who was not impressed by Kelly's development was his old friend Hugh Walpole, whose portrait Kelly had begun as early as 1914, and whom he continued to paint at intervals after the war. By 1926 he had completed three portraits of Walpole. But 'somehow, somewhere', as Kelly wrote to Walpole's biographer Rupert Hart-Davis, 'Hugh learned that I was a photographic painter, academic in the worst sense of that word, and surely no man of sensibility could tolerate my pompous productions. So Hugh was in a fix, and, bless him, how clumsy he was!' Walpole eventually managed to convey to Kelly that he did not want to own one of his portraits. At the same time he naïvely invited Kelly to approach Augustus John and ask him if he would do the job instead. Hart-Davis adds: 'This Kelly very graciously did,' an understatement in the circumstances.

Kelly was modest about his painting, and knew his limitations. He saw himself as a 'craftsman painter'. He found great joy in his art, not least in his off-duty landscapes. Kenneth Clark has summed him up as an artist in a letter to the author:

> I admired a great deal of his painting [writes Lord Clark]. The famous series of Eastern Dancers includes many pictures which I am sure will continue to give pleasure as long as anyone is allowed to enjoy painting. I also admire the best of his portraits, like the one of Almroth Wright and, of course, the early one of his father.* He had a great gift for summing up the character of his sitters, and painted with scrupulous honesty. Unfortunately the quality of his paint became rather uninteresting, and he very seldom achieved the kind of simplification which underlies even the most naturalistic-looking portraits of his beloved Ingres. But when all is said he was the most reliable portrait painter of his time, and for that reason I recommended him to paint the royal portraits of George VI and Queen Elizabeth.

* Plate 2.

2

It is time to mention an important influence on Kelly's life and art – his contemporary Alan Beeton, A.R.A. (1880–1942), of Charterhouse and Trinity College, Cambridge, whom he met in Paris in the early years of the century. An artist of independent means and outlook, Beeton acquired a magnificent technique, his style evolving in the direction of extreme realism. The larger pictures were portraits and figure studies; he also painted still-lifes from a lay-figure and, most amusingly, children's toys. His output was small, but his distinction deserves more recognition than it has received. Kelly bought several of Beeton's pictures (one for £350) and used to keep some of them in his studio to inspire his craftsmanship.

Kelly's letters to Beeton show affectionate admiration for this neglected artist. He went out of his way to recommend his work, rejoiced at his successes, and was helpful in securing his election as A.R.A. in 1938. When Kelly in the nineteen-sixties organized a travelling exhibition called 'A Painter's Choice', he made Beeton the main attraction, including twenty-five of his pictures (others represented being Allan Gwynne-Jones, Kenneth Newton, and Annie Swynnerton).

At the most critical moment of the Second World War, Kelly was to write to Beeton: 'It is a grim look out. I have been very fond of you for a very long time so I'll put on record that you have given me much pleasure. Thanks!' After this, it will seem churlish to suggest that Beeton's influence on Kelly may not have been altogether for the good, and that Beeton's example encouraged excessive literalism.

3

Kelly's Academy portraits of the nineteen-twenties ranged from the Principal of Cheltenham Ladies' College and Viscount Chelmsford to the Bishop of Rochester and the Masters of two Cambridge Colleges. He was made A.R.A. in 1922, and in 1924 he went with Jane to New York to undertake several American commissions. They eventually stayed for nine months, but Kelly did not enjoy it and found his living expenses enormous. Perhaps the most successful of his American pictures was his portrait of 'Katherine Francis' – Spanish-looking, with rich browns and yellows – exhibited at the Academy in 1926. She became a famous film actress, who years later wrote to Kelly:

> . . . 'Shades of 1925' – How kind you were to me when I came to your studio on Central Park S. – but also – you frightened me most to death when you said 'One day you are pink – One day you are yellow – Why does your skin tone change?' Do you remember? – So many years have passed & now you are Sir Gerald & I am Kay Francis. (16 September 1959.)

There was a slackening in the correspondence between Kelly and Maugham during the early nineteen-twenties. Both men were now married, but while Kelly's marriage was happy, his friend's was the reverse. Maugham spent much of his time travelling restlessly over the world, writing and collecting material. In 1928, after his divorce, he bought the Villa Mauresque at Cap Ferrat, where he established a permanent base. At once he turned to Kelly for advice on furnishing and decorating his property. Maugham was grateful to Kelly for the gift of two sadaiks (Burmese chests decorated with small pieces of mirror) to ornament his patio, and in 1929 he wrote that he had had 'the three pictures you gave me framed and put up in the hall and they look grand'.

It was their mutual interest in art that now chiefly kept the friendship alive; but this bond was strong, and founded in imperishable memories. Kelly influenced Maugham considerably in the gathering of his splendid art collection; Maugham owned three still-lifes by Roderick O'Conor, for example, whom he had met in Paris on Kelly's introduction, while his interest in the Impressionists and in Gauguin stemmed largely from Kelly's advocacy. One might have said the same of Maugham's famous collection of theatrical pictures, except that Maugham probably first noticed the art of Zoffany and de Wilde on the walls of the Garrick Club.

By 1930, when he was elected R.A., Kelly had established a reputation at the Academy, not merely as a painter, but also as an art enthusiast with potentialities as administrator, organizer, and educator. He was soon appointed one of the visitors who periodically examined and instructed in the Painting School. A report dated 25 November 1930 has survived in the files of the Academy. In it Kelly urged the creation of a class for 'still life'. 'The study of a still-life can continue, easily, for a longer period,' he wrote, 'than is possible in the case of a nude or draped model, and thus students could be introduced to the increasing difficulties which arise in completing a canvas that is destined to become a finished picture.' He found the students 'indulgent of my foibles and very pleasant and well behaved', attributing the improvement in discipline 'since last I was a visitor' to 'Mr Russell's work'.*

Kenneth Clark observed three great qualities in Kelly. These were his love of art; his reverence for the great artists he had known in his youth; his own personal gifts as an artist. Lord Clark's opinion of him as a painter has already been noted, but the same letter deserves further quotation:

> First of all [Lord Clark writes], he was a sincere and passionate lover of art, with a remarkably good eye. I remember one or two small exhibitions that he organized before the war of pictures by relatively unknown artists which had a personal appeal to him. They could have been done only by someone with a real eye for painting and an unprejudiced mind. Like all people who really love a subject he could never have enough of it. He was like Yehudi Menuhin who cannot stop playing the violin, or Myra Hess who could not stop playing the piano.

When he refers to Kelly's first attempts to organize exhibitions, Lord Clark may have in mind his 'Anthology' exhibition in the autumn of 1931, which opened at Cambridge and then came to London. The twenty contributors to Kelly's 'Anthology' included Duncan Grant and Matthew Smith, as well as older artists like Rothenstein, Clausen, Sickert, Tonks, and Steer. The artist whom Kelly most wished to please, and whom he chiefly consulted, was Henry Tonks (1862–1937).

So modest was Tonks that he 'quite genuinely believed', in the words of his biographer, William Hone, 'that his contribution was being invited as a kindness. When he discovered that Kelly did truly admire his work, his delight was like that of a child. His gratitude was unbounded.'

The 'Anthology' exhibition cheered Tonks's later years. Kelly's concern for the old man was typical of him. It was Kelly who took the lead in organizing financial help for James Pryde (1866–1941), when Pryde was living in sordid poverty in the last years of his life. Thanks largely to Kelly's efforts, the Council of the Royal Academy granted Pryde a Turner annuity and the State awarded him a Civil List pension. 'It was always an odd feeling, especially when one had been struggling with his water rate,' wrote Kelly to Pryde's biographer, 'to meet the old chap himself who, in spite of the waste and the vanities, was so genial, so

---

* Later Sir Walter Russell, Keeper of the Royal Academy Schools, 1927–42.

wise and witty, and, to cap all, so profoundly distinguished in appearance. I had, as you may recognize, a very real affection for him.' Kelly also did much to secure a Civil List pension for Walter Sickert (1860–1942).

This respect and consideration for older artists was innate in Kelly, and had already been shown in his admiration for the French geniuses he had met. His 'memory and reverence' for them impressed Kenneth Clark: 'It was really thrilling to talk to someone who had not only known Rodin and Monet (even I could have done that) but who had penetrated into the studio of Degas and been treated cordially. Gerald must have been a most charming young man.'

4

The secret is out – if it has ever been in question. Kelly was a charmer.

His was not a simple charm, however, but a complicated exposition of Irishness, in which abruptness contrasted with courtesy and delicacy of feeling. Unpretentious in manner, he took everyone as he found them. The pompous might be disconcerted by Kelly's directness; the professional art expert might be ruffled by a flat assertion of independent judgement and intuition. Kelly's gift of the gab could lead him to say too much. He could be petulant, tactless, bad-tempered. Yet in those who worked most closely with him, such as his secretaries, he inspired much affection. And, finally, his artistic integrity and the driving force of his lifelong passion were to bundle aside the doubts and criticisms – legitimate though many of them were – and make Kelly one of the most vigorous and effective champions of art in twentieth-century England.

Kelly's success as portrait painter and impresario had the immediate effect of depriving Jane of a personal maid. Instead, her husband found that he had to engage a long series of secretaries; and he bought a Remington typewriter which gave them good service for many years. On 4 February 1932, he apologized for the 'typewriting' to his friend William Hutton Riddell (1880–1947) – the painter of wild life, who lived in Spain – and went on to tell him something about the organization of his 'Anthology' exhibition:

> I had a great success both in Cambridge and in London but the labour entailed in getting these Exhibitions together was simply enormous. I started in a very amateurish fashion by writing letters

in my own fair hand and having them written on this noble typewriter, and I found that each picture that I got easily represented
some two letters of mine and two of the owners, while those that
were coy and difficult cost sometimes as much as six or eight! As
soon as the success at Cambridge was noticeable, it was decided
to pass it on to London, and a letter had to be written to every
owner before that could be arranged!

Kelly writes here with some sense of surprise at the ardours of
organizing exhibitions. Twenty years later, he was to know the procedure only too well. But the endless letter-writing and dictation that
lay before him was never to be taken for granted. His letters were
sparkling, stylish, enjoyable as his talk. He took pains to make them
personal to the recipient by inserting openings and endings, and by
correcting the typing in his own graceful hand. Nothing but the best
would do; whether he was helping a fellow artist; coaxing a valued
painting from a cautious owner; or sending a long informative answer
to an unknown inquirer.

It was no coincidence that Kelly's income increased after his mar-
riage; he now had an incentive to make a successful career. Mrs Mary
Delgado remembers being painted by him, as a child of four, in 1923.
Kelly became impatient when she blinked while he was painting her
eyes, and Mary burst into tears. 'Take her home, nurse,' he said firmly.
The fee for that portrait was £150.

Nine years later, someone was ready to spend ten times that amount
on a Kelly portrait. In his letter of 1932 to W. H. Riddell, Kelly
wrote:

> . . . I have had a few nasty jars including the sad story of the
> American lady who had agreed to pay me the not inconsiderable
> sum of fifteen hundred guineas for a portrait (you will perceive at
> once that she is not, perhaps, very sensible), but alas she does not
> seem to have been able to take the ordinary precautions in life and
> on meeting a motor car had three ribs broken. This was in Paris,
> and she promptly returned to New York to have them mended. I
> do not think it is worth my while bringing an action against the
> driver of the motor, but it was a depressing business altogether.

The American lady had been a disappointment, it is true, but Kelly's
fees now fluctuated, somewhat unpredictably, and according to circumstances, between the extremes indicated by these two portraits. With
some private means, and with a flow of sitters that increased steadily,

Kelly at fifty was comfortably off. This was just as well, for he had extravagant tastes. He and Jane travelled abroad regularly, often to Portofino and to Abano, near Padua, where he took the mud baths for arthritis; they also visited Maugham at Cap Ferrat. But Kelly tended to prefer busman's holidays; much of his time was spent sketching and painting out of doors.

5

In the winter of 1930–31, Dr Frederick W. Hilles of Yale was in London studying the Boswell Papers, while his wife sat to Kelly for her portrait. Dr Hilles had already edited the *Letters* of Sir Joshua Reynolds and later he wrote a book on Reynolds's *Literary Career*. He was in a mood to Boswellize: to discover a modern successor to the first President of the Royal Academy. On 24 November 1930, he recorded that he had been struck with the 'wit, charm, personality' of Kelly and held 'spellbound by his rapid talk'. Kelly was 'stocky, well-built, wore a loose-fitting gray sweater (which was stretched because one hand is always in a pocket) and a pair of loose gray bags. He talks . . . like a blue streak, gesticulates as he does so . . . and as he talks fixes you with keen eyes.'

Hilles and his wife dined with the Kellys on 15 December 1930, to meet H. M. Harwood, the playwright, and his wife F. Tennyson Jesse, whom Hilles described in his diary as 'blonde with a hard face & a tremendous sense of her own importance in things intellectual', while Harwood was 'the reverse of his wife as far as appearance & temperament is concerned. Solid, dark, quiet, dignified, thoroughly likeable.' The diary continues:

> . . . Our host was not present when we arrived, nor did he put in his appearance until we had been present for some time. This I discover is quite characteristic. Either he is in his cellar picking out wines or in his studio sketching. A maid is sent to him every five minutes to tell him how late it is, and he always answers cheerfully that he is just finishing, but he nevertheless continues his work . . .
>
> I am disgusted that I didn't run away with the menu. The food was delicious. One dish was pheasant, cut up and cooked en casserole? in a sauce made of marron which had been soaked in something like Madeira for some time. G. & Jane had shelled the

nuts themselves. The food was delicious, but the wines were positively amazing. There were, I think, seven in all. The first few were not particularly rare, but as we progressed they became more & more so. One bottle had been placed in his grandmother's cellar in '64. . . .

19 December 1930 . . . We arrived in the studio at 4. G.K. was not in evidence – 'in the wine cellar' he later explained. When Sue [Mrs Hilles] said he seemed more devoted to his cellar than anything else, he replied 'I have three passions in life: 1. Painting, 2. Jane, 3. Wine' – and apparently in that order. Jane entertained us as we awaited him. We were amused to find the sitter's chair occupied by a dummy clothed in an old fur coat. On the easel was an almost finished portrait of a very distinguished elderly lady clad in a fur coat. We wondered whether the original would be pleased to know that the dummy was taking her place. Jane said one never realizes when one sees the finished portrait what actually took place while it was being painted. 'You remember,' said she, 'the diploma picture, Jane XXX?* Everyone said how wealthy the Kellys must be – look at the gorgeous clothes she is wearing.' Actually Jane bought three or four yards of velvet, and attached it to a fur collar belonging to a friend of hers. G.K. wished to paint moiré; she had no moiré dress and so bought a yard of it which she made into a strap that appears over the cloak.

In a letter written home on 21 December 1930, Hilles re-affirmed that the Kellys were 'delightful'. He went on:

> I am hypnotized by Gerald . . . He has a quick tongue and is one of those rare mortals who can say something ordinary in a new and original way. Jane is lovely to look upon, especially when clad in white . . . She is small, blonde, quiet, but can talk well when she should. She made an excellent hostess . . . Gerald is such an easy talker that I never know when to believe him, but I am now convinced that whatever he is he is not a poseur.

The diary adds: 'Over Xmas I happened to see a *Who's Who* & looked up G.K. who I found was born 51 years ago, which is astonishing. I had mentally placed him as being 10 years younger.'

31 December 1930 . . . I had work to do, so did not accompany Sue to the studio in the morning. He had expected to start sketching her head. Actually he quarrelled with her over the material

* Plate 8b.

she had finally chosen, saying it was too light for her eyes . . . It
was a dark morning, so instead of painting her he suggested they
go to the Wallace Collection . . . They went & he showed her his
idea of the finest female portrait of all time, Velasquez's 'Woman
with a Fan'. . . .

5 *January 1931* . . . I was shown Rosie's portrait,* which though
now being redone is still a lovely thing. He showed me the picture
of it as it was first and as it was after he'd shellaced it. Then
recently it went bad. The skirt marbled and a spot appeared on her
neck; he therefore decided to restore it if possible. His friends
have told him it is impossible, he'll only ruin a good picture, but
he's going to try it anyhow. Rosie, or rather Sue, stands with a
queenly pose. Her face is very refined, soft. A boa is wound round
her right arm. We told G.K. of the review in the *Tatler* which said
the flaw in the book was Rosie, that such a character was in-
credible. G.K. said she was painted by Maugham exactly as in life.
That he M. had come to Paris & told G.K. he was desperately in
love with a female who wasn't much to look at, but he'd like her
portrait. She came of common family – her mother was particularly so – and had married at the age of 19 not because she was
in love but because her sister was engaged & she wished to get
ahead of her . . . She led a miserable life . . . & then met Willie,
the only man she ever really loved, thinks G.K. This did not keep
her from continuing her promiscuous ways . . . Maugham hasn't
changed her a bit. He has no compunctions about the feelings of
people. She is still alive. G.K. said M. shouldn't put her in. He
replied that no one would know but the four or five who themselves are in the book. He said that the book dealt with the period
G.K. knew intimately. That now he & Willie saw little of each
other . . . They could talk about old times but one couldn't do
that for long . . . But *Cakes and Ale* was his Willie. He watched
the whole Rosie episode from start to finish. . . .

I asked him what the shortest time he ever spent on a portrait
was. He replied five days, & it was 'the best likeness I ever got' –
an old lady† – but he added it was never really finished. He maintained however that he wasn't a slow painter, that it took him
days to find a pose he liked. Often he took many photos of his
sitter & found one in that way. Once he had begun the rest was

* i.e. Kelly's portrait of 'Sue' (Ethelwyn Sylvia Jones), the original of Rosie in
Maugham's *Cakes and Ale*, then recently published.
† Perhaps Mrs Harrison. D.H.

easy. He found the face the least interesting. 'I always know I'll have to do a lot of work on it and that people will look at the face and nothing else, but personally I get much more pleasure out of the rest.' He muttered later on something to the effect that a likeness was an elusive thing. He had made Sue's [Mrs Hilles's] upper lip too large & the nose was slightly at an angle. After 20 minutes or so he had altered this & the likeness was surprisingly good.

Dancing was mentioned. He's not one who likes it, though Jane does. He once asked Arthur Balfour if he danced. No, he said, I prefer to do my walking unimpeded by a member of the opposite sex. . . .

He said: 'I am interested in this Victorian poet everyone is talking about.' I asked what his name was. He couldn't remember & rang for the maid. Ruth or Constance answered. But after some wait. He said in a firm & irritated voice 'You'll have to learn to answer the bells more promptly. Bring me the Times Lit. Supp. Any issue you can find.' She returned soon with it & the first communication was from Charles Williams, editor of this man's poems, answering his critics. G.K. then turned to the maid & said . . . 'Get the phone no. of B———.' She returned in a moment. 'The book dealers?' 'Yes.' When she had left he said 'That is the first time she has shown any glimmering of intelligence today.' When she gave him the no. he went to the phone, asked for one of the men in the shop by name, gave the name of the poet (which escapes me),* the name of the editor, & added 'Have you got it? Send me a copy.' He is very abrupt on the phone. He uses no words more than necessary, cryptic. . . .

While he painted he held in his left hand a stick, long with a padded end. Sue asked why. 'To support my enfeebled hand,' he answered. He apparently rested the padded end on the easel or lower part of the canvas. Every once in a while he'd leave his position, remarking half humorously & chiefly to himself, 'I want the largest brush you can give me.' . . . This he'd use on her hair, the smaller brushes for the face. . . .

6 January 1931 . . . In the a.m. we went to the private view of the Persian Exhibition.† G.K. had said yesterday that he liked going because he saw all his old cronies there. We found him in the 3rd gallery with an elderly gent & wife. They were looking at a carpet in the middle of the room on the floor . . . I don't know what he

---

* Gerard Manley Hopkins. D.H.   † At Burlington House.

Rose Kelly, sister of Gerald Kelly.

The Kellys after their marriage at St Michael's, Paddington, on 15 April 1920:
(*seated*) Jane Kelly, (*standing*) Ivor Back, wearing top hat, and next to him
(*right*) Kelly's sister Rose; (*at rear, with hand raised*) Geoffrey Toye, (*at right*)
Gerald's mother, and Gerald.

was saying but he was talking rapidly & pointing at various parts of it as he talked. He looked rather old today, the face in repose shows he has led a nervous life . . . He bowed at us very politely & formally. . . .

9 January 1931 . . . Sue spent the day (until tea time) at the studio . . . Much of the time was devoted to taking pictures of her in various attitudes. The rest of the time he worked a bit on the background & much on the face. He moved her nose now one way, now another. . . .

21 January 1931 . . . Took Sue to studio at 11. Found he had had the photo enlarged, marked off like a graph, & transferred to the canvas . . . I asked him if he always graphed his portraits . . . He said Sickert always did – that he did very seldom. He did it with this because we are behindhand in this case & it saves time. . . .

22 January 1931 . . . He showed me a letter Rudyard Kipling wrote him several weeks ago from Bath, starting off 'Dear Kelly'* . . . I asked where he had met Kipling. He said the Beefsteak Club. That he had sat next to him there & had had a most interesting talk. That Kipling was very witty, & not at all spoiled by success. He told G.K. he had to hide on Sundays from the curious – that he was annoyed by high prices paid for fair copies he had made – the money of course not going to him. He needs no money, however, his only son being killed in the war. He still tries to write well – has no feeling that because he has made his reputation he can rest. . . .

G.K. said [to Kipling] he was about to go to the R.A. to teach the children how to paint. Kipling said 'For a tuppence I'd join you.' 'Well,' said G.K., 'Here's the tuppence.' 'No,' said Kipling, 'it would get in the press.' 'Nonsense, when you walk in, eighty per cent of the students would recognize you & would behave admirably. You could then ask them to say nothing.' But Kipling wouldn't go. . . .

G.K. wears a funny broad-brimmed hat without the crown to shade his eyes. Otherwise the light gets behind his spectacles & makes it hard for him to see clearly. Jane wouldn't let it be a complete hat for fear he would go bald.

10 February 1931 . . . I called for Sue and was amazed at the change in the portrait. It looks very much more complete. He said

---

* Lady Kelly has allowed me to read this letter of Rudyard Kipling's of 6 January 1931, and another of 17 October 1931. In both letters Kipling regretfully refuses invitations from Kelly to convivial occasions.

he would be through this week, which he isn't, but at least it is
coming along well. I think he likes it. . . .

13 February 1931 . . . Yesterday Sue sat in tears because of a tiff
with me the previous night. He was very sympathetic, got her a
cup of tea to soothe her, and gave her plenty of good advice, and
had lunch with her . . . He said he & Jane never let the sun go
down on their anger. That however mad at each other they might
be, they always made it up before going to bed. He was amused
that Sue could tell him things she couldn't tell me. He scolded her
for hitting me with a hot-water bottle. He chose today of all days
to repaint her face, when she was looking badly because of no
sleep. . . .

I noticed today in the R.A. that G.K. is this year a member of
the Council – his first year in that capacity. With him are Augustus
John, Bill Orpen,* & several others equally distinguished.

6

The extracts from Dr Hilles's diary represent only a small part of what
he wrote. It was a tribute to Kelly's personality that such a scholarly
observer should have been so carried away. The portrait of Mrs Hilles
duly appeared in the Academy exhibition of 1931.

During this period a much younger portrait-painter, the Scotsman
James Gunn (1893–1964) was making his mark at the Academy summer
shows. Kelly and Gunn were competitors, but they also had a common
interest in that indigent Scottish genius, James Pryde. It was para-
doxical that two such methodical practitioners should have shared a
compassionate admiration for a painter of romantic fantasy (who once
objected to a certain portrait because it was 'too like a face').

Gunn's reputation was founded on his excellent portraits of Pryde.
In 1933 his portrait of Delius was the Academy 'picture of the year'.
Many thought the Royal Academy surprisingly tardy in recognizing
Gunn's qualities, despite the unevenness of his work. However, he was
eventually elected an Associate in 1953, during Kelly's presidency.

Meanwhile, in 1933, Kelly's 'The Jester' – the portrait of Maugham
painted in 1911 – was seen again at the Academy's summer exhibition
on its purchase for the Tate Gallery under the Chantrey Bequest.
Maugham wrote to tell him he had received as many letters of congratulation as if he 'had just been delivered of a son & heir'. In the 1934

* Sir William Orpen, R.A., died in this year, 1931.

Academy, Kelly's portrait of Sir Almroth Wright, at his bench in the old Inoculation Department at St Mary's Hospital, Paddington, made a great impression.

So much work was coming in that assistants were now needed in Gloucester Place; they were conveniently found among those who had studied at the Royal Academy Schools. In 1934 John Frye Bourne, having finished his time as a student, went to work for Kelly three days a week to 'learn a good studio technique'. He used to arrive at 9.00 a.m., and began by 'preparing' the paint left over from the previous day and transferring it to a clean palette. Then he might start work on a canvas, if he knew what he was supposed to do; but he had first to clean the surface of any atmospheric dirt or grease by swabbing with cotton-wool dipped in methylated spirit – Kelly's meticulous craftsmanship leaving nothing to chance. Bourne assisted Kelly on his portrait of Dr M. R. James, the Provost of Eton. For this picture, part of the wall and bookshelves of the Provost's study at Eton were reproduced in the studio by a carpenter, and his books were on the shelves. Kelly preferred to work with the actual background whenever he could.

After what Bourne judged, from the distant sound and smell, to have been a splendid breakfast, Kelly appeared in the studio between ten o'clock and ten-thirty. He removed his jacket, unbuttoned the remarkable 'half-sleeves' of his shirt – his own invention – and, laying these aside, put on his blue smock.

According to Bourne, it was the custom in 1934 for a maid to bring in an enormous silver tea-pot, etc., and a huge fruit cake at about one o'clock, and do exactly the same again at four o'clock. Apart from these intervals for refreshment, work continued until five-thirty or six o'clock. Certain of Kelly's friends used to come into the studio and talk – among them Somerset Maugham, who sometimes also occupied the sitter's chair (Plate 10a).

> I remember [writes Mr Bourne] a typical conversation about a forthcoming visit by Mr Maugham to the studio of Mr Algernon Newton. Mr Newton's works consisted – invariably so far as I know – of rather pleasing scenes of evening sunlight on trees & buildings. Having seen one there could be little new to say about the others. Mr Maugham & Mr Kelly discussed, with some merriment, the various words & phrases which could serve the call of politeness.
> . . . Mr Kelly, being a small man, had a pugnacious disposition, as so often happens. I was six-foot-two & painfully thin. On one

occasion this contrast of size resulted in a rather amusing incident. A new portrait was being begun – I don't remember of whom – & a squared-up photograph was being transferred to the canvas. Mr Kelly called me from what I was doing to work with him. I stood directly behind him & drew from the top downwards while he worked from the bottom up. Mr Kelly kept up a tirade about my inaccuracy – not that my line was wrong, but that I would work 'by eye' & not 'by measurement'. Mr Kelly himself was extremely careful in checking everything to the hundredth part of a square. I admit I was very impatient with this method. I recall that the gentleman in the portrait wore a bow-tie & I was approaching that article with my line. But it was obvious that Mr Kelly's line & mine were not going to meet – one of us was *a whole square* out! I reassured myself the culprit wasn't me, but I hadn't the courage to say anything, especially as I was still being abused for inaccuracy. However the discrepancy soon became obvious & Mr Kelly called out, 'Oh my God! – is it *you* or is it *me*??'

It was the work of a moment for him to see that he was in error. 'Damn!' he said, and, throwing down the charcoal, he left the studio.

Kelly's mother lived until 1935. After her death he received his remaining share of the family fortune and in 1936 embarked on a world tour with Jane. He painted landscapes in China and Cambodian ladies in Phnom-Penh; and he told his interrogators on the radio programme 'Frankly Speaking' that seeing Angkor Wat – the ruined sacred city of Cambodia – in the moonlight was the most vivid memory of his life.

The Kellys returned to London in 1937, to find Gerald had lost a large sum of money, unwisely invested on his behalf by a friend in a business that failed. It was a serious blow which meant he had to paint harder than ever. Fortunately there was no lack of sitters. He now fixed his fee for a portrait at a thousand guineas.

Students who encountered Kelly as a visiting teacher at the Royal Academy Schools had mixed memories of the experience. Kelly thought there were too many art students. He belonged to the old school of teachers of music or art who believed in plain-speaking and hard-hitting. Students had to be both talented and persevering if they were to receive any encouragement from him.

Heda Berkeley was one whose work interested him, and whom he invited to his studio. 'I remember getting a five-hour berating from him after one of the student exhibitions for a travelling scholarship,' she writes.

No student *now* would put up with what we had to! . . . All the same, Kelly cared about painting, and was ready to help . . . He measured heads for portraits with callipers, as a sculptor might. He gave me a pair, he gave me several useful things, besides advice about painting. None of his gifts were ever wrapped either in tissue paper or pretty words. When he attended to a person it was like a searchlight halting upon an object. The glare of it was both flattering and hard to bear. He was so interested in what you were that he made no attempt to impress you about himself in any way whatever. I never saw him make use of disdain, any more than a child would.

Kelly said to her once:

'You won't paint anything worth looking at until you're past forty, well past.'

I was dismayed, being only twenty-one.

'You're so bloody immature, it will take a long time. You might even turn out to be a better artist than I am.'

Pause, then – 'and that's saying nothing because I'm no artist'.

'What are you?' feeling I was perhaps talking to a lunatic.

'A painter' – and then he would expound upon what that meant.

He favoured the finest possible texture in a canvas, with the smallest 'tooth' to it – calling the accidental effects of the rough type, cheating. Nor would transparent scumblings left as shadows from the first painting be called other than cheating. 'Paint it, damn you,' he would shout, hopping about in a rage. . . .

Then he sent for tea, beautiful fragrant tea he had brought with him from the East, and said 'Pour out. No sugar, no milk – you must learn what's what.'

Afterwards he would bring out a picture, perhaps it would be a Monet, and talk about how it was done and what Monet was thinking of at the time, and how much better it was than anything he could do, and get on with his copy of it, and send me away without turning his head or saying goodbye, already lost in what he was doing.

Heda Berkeley was asked by the curator of the Academy Schools whether she would like to become Kelly's assistant; but she thought this was something for John Napper, her first husband, rather than herself. Napper assisted Kelly from 1937 to 1939, and was more of an apprentice than an employee. He stresses the importance in Kelly's technique of the grinding of colours by hand. It was only by having his colours ground under his supervision that Kelly could be sure the right oil, in the right quantity, would go into each colour, and that the amount of grinding would be regulated. Napper not only ground all Kelly's colours, but also prepared his canvases, filtered oils, spirits and essences, and made mediums, glues for *marouflage*, paint removers, and a host of chemical compounds which Kelly preferred to have manufactured under his eye than supplied to him from outside.

Kelly's practice of using photographs as an initial aid, in order to save time, was now firmly established. Napper deplored it as restricting, especially as 'he was perfectly able to draw as well as most – and much better than some.' Indeed, the results when Kelly used no camera were the same as when he did, only they took much longer to achieve.

Napper would work on a background, or a chair, or tassels for a Lord Chamberlain's gown, or even pose for the hand of a Chancellor of the Exchequer (Sir John Simon's portrait was then being painted, to hang in the National Liberal Club).

> People would be in and out of the studio, and conversation flowed like a sparkling river [writes John Napper]. G.K. said to me during my first week 'My boy – it's no use you sitting silently in your corner. If you are ever to become a painter you've got to learn to talk while you work – you'll get nowhere if you don't!' And he certainly knew how to use his very quick and witty mind whilst at the same time concentrating completely on the work going on on his canvas. I used to enjoy the sittings when he was engaged upon one of his many portraits of Somerset Maugham; being friends of a life-time, they talked together in a way that only old friends can.
>
> The painters he liked most were Ingres, Claude Monet, and his friend Alan Beeton, a very remarkable painter.
>
> He told me how one evening he was walking with a friend in Montmartre when he met Picasso. The friend (who knew Picasso) asked him to join them over a 'pot'. Picasso replied that he was in a hurry as he was going to have a bath. They parted and went their ways. Some moments later hurrying footsteps were heard behind them, and Picasso caught them up in order to tell them that he

was *not*, in fact, on his way to have a bath. Having delivered himself of this, he again went off into the night, free of the lie he had told in order to 'épater' the Englishman.

G.K. had a violent side to his nature, especially in those days. I remember when he chased one of the best frame-makers in the country round the studio! On the other hand, he could be remarkably kind and helpful to friends in need.

Often he would work on through the lunch hour, stopping only for a sandwich. His slow painstaking methods made sure that there was always work in hand in the studio: portraits, landscapes, Burmese dancers, still-lives, started sometimes many years previously, would be got out, washed down, worked on, put away, and so on. Technically it was sound, emotionally it was a little too 'controlled' – and yet this discipline is lacking in so much contemporary art, and I think that somewhere there is a happy balance to be found. One thing I am sure about: his works will survive better than most of his contemporaries' from the standpoint of chemistry and method.

Tea-time in the studio was a pleasant interval of relaxation. Kelly would tell his secretary and Napper stories or inventions, and sometimes he would read to them. Two hours later, Napper had to do his 'most hated job' – washing the brushes. Kelly had phases when he was so obsessed by 'cleanness of colour' that he would make one mark with a brush, put it down, take up another brush, and so on throughout the day.

On some nights, Napper had between 200 and 300 brushes to wash. Yet, exasperating as it was, he admits that the discipline greatly helped him in his own career as a painter. Nearly forty years later, he still uses brushes which Kelly gave him in the thirties.

John Napper was with him when he was commissioned to paint the State Portraits of King George VI and Queen Elizabeth. It was an undertaking which dominated Kelly's efforts for several years to come.

CHAPTER SIX

The State Portraits

I

When a new Sovereign comes to the throne it has for centuries been customary for the State to commission an official portrait of the successor together with one of his consort. A master-copy of each used to be made, so that numerous replicas might be hand-painted to hang in Government Houses and Embassies overseas. In recent years the procedure has been simplified by the use of colour-printed facsimiles.

At the beginning of the Second World War, large portraits of King Edward VII and Queen Alexandra, and of King George V and Queen Mary, were hanging in the entrance hall of Government House, Hong Kong. Their fate might have been thought precarious when the house was occupied by the enemy for several years; but such was the veneration of the Japanese for the principle of monarchy that they encased the portraits in teak containers and moved them to the security of the basement. Queen Victoria presented a graver problem. Enthroned in marble and mounted on a massive pedestal, she dominated the long ballroom. Her courteous captors built a brick wall around her, considerately leaving a slit before her eyes. All of which shows that State Portraits must be taken seriously.

Kelly was commissioned to paint the State Portraits of King George VI and Queen Elizabeth (Plate 8a) in 1938, on the recommendation of Sir Kenneth Clark as Surveyor of the King's Pictures. They were to be about 9 feet high and nearly 6 feet wide. Intended to hang in the private apartments at Windsor Castle, they were not completed until 1945. Kelly left his own short account of their painting:

> In due course I went to Windsor and stayed for a night or two with Their Majesties. There were difficulties: I hadn't seen the

Coronation, and the King didn't like wearing his coronation clothes. He dressed well and wore his everyday suits with ease and distinction, and I was told that uniform presented no problems to him; but I think it might be said of the coronation costume that it was almost a stage garment, it wasn't really a uniform. It consisted of a full-skirted coat of mauve-violet satin with some lines of gold braid under which could just be seen the white satin riding breeches and white silk stockings. He put these on, but he was self-conscious and uncomfortable. I had to try and solve the problem of persuading this modest man to strike some decorative pose, because I had got it firmly into my head that a State Portrait should be romantically decorative. The King was infinitely patient. He didn't like posing and he didn't pose for long, but he did pose frequently.

Then came the difficulty of the background. After a lot of trials I had an ingenious idea and I got my friend Sir Edwin Lutyens* to make me a decorative set in the manner of the palace at Delhi, and he did it exactly as I wanted it. That is to say, there was a shadow behind the light side of the King's head and illumination on the wall behind the part of the head that was in shadow. A small model was made (by the same craftsman who had made Queen Mary's doll's house) and a little figure of proper size. . . .

The Queen was a different story. It is hard to suggest the admiration and affection which grew all around her. From wherever one looked at her, she looked nice: her face, her voice, her smile, her skin, her colouring – everything was right. (Foreword to catalogue of touring exhibition of his Royal Portrait Sketches, circulated 1961.)

The portrait of the King was the first to be begun, and John Napper remembers posing in the coronation costume in the studio in Gloucester Place. A study of the head and hands of the King's picture was painted at Windsor in April 1939. Kelly made sketches of the Queen in October 1938 and January 1939. There were many difficulties, as always with such huge official commissions, especially for an artist so meticulous about accuracy; and from the beginning the backgrounds worried him. He and Jane decided not to pay their usual visit to Italy in 1939, but, as he wrote to W. H. Riddell on 22 August, 'to dedicate my

---

* Lutyens had designed not only Viceroy's House, Delhi, but also Queen Mary's doll's house at Windsor Castle. He was President of the Royal Academy from 1938 until his death in 1944.

time to finishing off those confounded pictures'. However, he was tempted by an invitation to stay at the Lutyens-built Greywalls, Gullane, where a game of golf 'brings home how old one is getting'. Kelly was sixty – and war appeared inevitable: 'It looks as if anything may happen and most beastly things too.' Yet the letter to Riddell concluded cheerfully:

> Ned Lutyens has at last come up to scratch and has produced the most lovely design for H.M. portrait. It is a shallow coved archway with beautifully designed ashlar and some fine string coursing in marble too, which makes a really exquisite surface pattern as well as an architectural ensemble which gives me the shade and the light where I want it. This has been stolen from Delhi and in the Queen's portrait I propose to paint a little more of the same part of the Palace. This will be even more ingenious than using the same background for both of them.

On 25 August 1939, Kelly wrote to Sir Alexander Hardinge, the King's private secretary, to ask for advice as to what he should do if war broke out. He was told that his canvases should be taken to Windsor Castle for safety. This was done, and Kelly himself went to stay with his old friend Sir Henry Marten, the Vice-Provost of Eton, in order to complete the paintings. The following reminiscence by John Dugdale, then an Eton boy, belongs to this period:

> My father used to stay with Henry Marten when visiting me at Eton. One Sunday morning I went there to breakfast and Sir Gerald was staying with Sir Henry and painting the King and Queen at Windsor. Anyway, for some reason, after breakfast, Sir Gerald and I spent a quarter of an hour together in the dark hall at the foot of the stairs, he sitting on a chest, swinging his legs. 'What do you read?' I mumbled something. 'Do you read Somerset Maugham?' 'He's just a name.' So off he went about Maugham. And I couldn't wait till Monday to get hold of Cakes and Ale.
>
> Completely unimportant; but instead of reading the Sunday papers, he was happy and interested enough to bother with an uncouth fifteen-year-old and talk at what must have been the top of his bent. It's always stuck in my mind.

Kelly was lost without a secretary. He found he now had to spend an hour a day writing letters in his own hand. 'It's a nuisance, a fearful burden,' he complained to Mrs Evelyn Harvey on 10 October, 'I'm not doing it very well.' Kelly was painting a portrait of her husband J. Craig Harvey, the East India merchant, an old friend of his, and he apologized profusely for the delay:

> I must stay put at Windsor until those pictures are done. The King's is practically finished (& looks rather noble!), I expect it'll be a month before the Queen's is through.
>
> Then, when my obligations to the Royal Family (!!ahem!!), are fulfilled I will at once proceed to deal with my obligations to you.

In the light of what was to follow, it seems incredibly optimistic of Kelly to have imagined he could finish the pictures before the end of 1939. Though his health had been generally excellent for many years, that autumn he was ill and upset. He told Mrs Harvey he had suffered from several feverish colds; and at Christmas, while on a visit to friends in Hertfordshire, he 'spent five miserable days in bed with a sort of 'flue.' By January 1940, he was writing to Mrs Harvey on Windsor Castle notepaper to say 'Tho' I am officially here to paint the Queen's portrait, I can & will come to Lainston to finish Craig's picture.' In May he was still hopeful, but thought he should choose the middle of a week for his visit. 'The week ends are my best chance of sittings from Their Majesties – who often come for the week end to Windsor.'

The portrait of Craig Harvey soon assumed almost as much importance in Kelly's mind as the pictures of the King and Queen. He had begun Harvey's portrait in 1938, when numerous photographs had been taken: 'Craig is what they call "photogenic" . . . This photogenic quality is a mystery. The King has it to a high degree, but the Queen is the opposite.' (13 December 1938.) By 1940 he was naturally under pressure from Mrs Harvey – who had paid half the fee of one thousand guineas – to get her picture finished. The strain of work on the State Portraits, the problems of wartime, and eventually the German bombing, drove Kelly distracted, and he only finished Craig Harvey's portrait by going to stay at his home, Lainston House, near Winchester, for several weeks in the autumn of 1940. Harvey gave him twenty-six sittings spread over three years; the background took seventeen days. 'I'm sure no picture caused more bother,' he wrote to Mrs Harvey, after his return to Windsor Castle to confront the huge royal canvases once again (2 December 1940):

I had a beautiful day for my drive here. The Castle across the Great Park was thought by Turner to be one of the loveliest views. It was once more an exquisite vision.

The pictures really look all right and, tho' you'll hardly credit it, they seemed pleased to see me back! H.M. has given me another & most interesting commission so I feel terrifically bucked! . . .

He left behind at Lainston his umbrella and a new silk tie, 'a brown one with diagonal stripes which I thought was rather natty'.

When he wrote to Mrs Harvey to thank her for forwarding these things (16 December 1940), he mentioned that Eton College had been bombed:

. . . Tho' the damage looked frightful (& I fear the whole façade of Upper School is now groggy) they are clearing it up & shoring it up – and of course we're lucky that the best bits haven't been touched.

The King has given me the job of making records – and I have got notes for three drawings. It's not exactly in my line but is tragically interesting to do.

2

Kelly had two good friends at Windsor Castle in Sir Alan Lascelles, who succeeded Hardinge as the King's private secretary, and Sir Owen Morshead, the Librarian. Sir Alan knew Kelly fairly well before he came to Windsor. They had a common acquaintance in Jasper Ridley, the Etonian banker who lived in Gloucester Place, and Kelly had painted a successful portrait of Lascelles' father-in-law, Lord Chelmsford. To Sir Alan the State Portraits seemed far advanced by the outbreak of war, and (according to Lascelles' recollection in 1974) Kelly requested only a few days' accommodation at the Castle in order to apply 'finishing touches'.

He was given a bedroom [writes Sir Alan Lascelles], & the use of one of the drawing-rooms for a studio. The 'few days' were expanded into the 'duration'. Officially, this was no concern of mine, but exclusively that of the Master of the Household; but I can recall the King making, in conversation, mild & semi-humorous protests at the length of his guest's visit. It was even

I had a beautiful day for my
drive here. The Castle across the
Great Park was thought by Turner
to be one of the loveliest views.
It was once more an exquisite
vision.
The pictures really look all right
and, tho' you'll hardly credit it,
they seemed pleased to see me
back!   H.M. has given me
another & most interesting
commission so I feel terrifically
bucked!

Let me repeat my apologies
for taking so much time over
Craig.

Yours

Gerald Kelly.

Sample of Kelly's handwriting

said, without foundation I think, that Gerald, like Penelope, got
up at night to undo the work he had done during the day. Personally, I was always delighted to find him still there, when I came
down to Windsor. I was based on London, & only went to
Windsor on an average of every other week-end. I enjoyed his
company at meals, & used often to make him join my afternoon
walk to Eton, etc. Sometimes, too, he would come with me to the
organ-loft in St. George's, where I often went to listen to my
friend Harris* playing the organ. I recall, too, his snatching up the

* Sir William Henry Harris.

poker in the Equerries' room, & giving us a vivid demonstration of the matador's art. . . .

Why did Kelly take so long over the royal portraits? Chiefly because he viewed them as the most important commissions of his life; indeed, they were the only works that he mentioned by name in his *Who's Who* entry. An absolute determination to make them a success alerted his complex apparatus of craftsmanship and, with it, his meticulous, almost pedantic, sense of accuracy.

The architectural background and the small model designed by Lutyens completely altered Kelly's ideas and plunged him into a whole series of fresh calculations. John Napper went off to the war, but for a time Kelly had Geoffrey Gleaves as his assistant on the pictures at Windsor:

> Neither of them is finished, [he wrote to Napper, 19 January 1941], tho' the King has got on a lot and the design of the Queen's picture is completed and a very complicated one it is. Without Gleaves' help I couldn't have made a good job of the perspective. Alone I should have had to rely on squaring up a photograph of the model.
>
> Of course you don't know of that model. Sir Edwin Lutyens designed a palace and a model ($\frac{1}{2}''$ to the foot) was made. We experimented with this and got good results. Then Gleaves and his wife laid down the vast canvas & proceeded to do a huge perspective drawing with real vanishing points 80 feet away!! The immense size of the room I paint in made this possible.

Seldom can a painter have worked in a saloon as palatial as that which formed Kelly's studio. It was, in fact, the Grand Reception Room to the State Apartments. Normally, the high walls were hung with a sequence of French tapestries, and the floor was spread with Aubusson carpets and set with giltwood settees; at the flick of a switch the massive candelabras would spring into light. But it was all quite different in wartime, when the room was stripped of its furnishings. In Sir Owen Morshead's words:

> Beneath the big North window, at his easel stood Mr Gerald Kelly, R.A., looking small.* Before him, 'boundless and bare,' the lone and level floor stretched far away. Its solitude he shared with two august lay-figures, shrouded in royal dust-sheets.

---

* He was 5 ft 6 in.

There was one other piece of furniture: Lutyens' doll's-size marble hall. A little King in coronation robes, and movable, stood on the black-and-white paving, his crown scintillating on a velvet cushion in the background. The model was placed beside the easel, at such a height that Kelly could study through a peep-hole the effects of light and shade, as well as the relation of the figure to its background.

Kelly occupied one of the top-storey bedrooms at the Castle, assigned to men visitors and served by a lift. He took his meals with members of the Royal Household. 'More often than not,' writes Sir Owen Morshead, 'in the improvised arrangements of war, the King and Queen would be at table too, together with the two Princesses and their governess, Miss Crawford. Buckingham Palace having been bombed [in September 1940], and St James's evacuated, the Castle was unwontedly full. In this assorted company he proved an enlivening ingredient, his copious conversation always fresh and not infrequently startling.' Kelly made a vivid impression on Princess Margaret, aged ten or eleven. After the war Kelly's cousin, Francis Toye, Director of the British Institute in Florence, had a conversation with her at the opera when she visited Italy. 'It wasn't about Monteverdi,' he wrote, 'it was about the idiosyncrasies of my distinguished P.R.A. cousin, Gerald Kelly, who would seem to have caused a regular flutter in the dovecots of Windsor Castle during his long residence.'

The nature of that 'regular flutter' is well suggested in an appraisal of Kelly published by *The Irish Times* (28 October 1950): 'He has not only the typical appearance of an Irishman (one incidentally which does not make you suspect his age) but that Irish informality which is neither obvious nor condescending, but entirely natural.'

3

'They were curious times at Windsor, were they not?' wrote Kelly to the Marquess of Hamilton long afterwards (23 July 1953). 'I made heavy weather over those State Portraits, but it is not an easy thing to paint pictures away from one's own studio, though there were of course compensations from time to time.'

The chief compensation was probably the proximity of Eton College. His noble studio overlooked its playing fields. Kelly had a genuine love, transcending snobbery, for the place, its buildings, and his friends there. Of course he appreciated the honour and advantages of living as the King's guest in the Castle which he had painted as a boy in 1897 (Plate 1b), but he worked hard to justify his presence.

In 1940–41 the King decided to re-arrange the pictures in the Garter Throne Room, and Kelly was commissioned to do two new portraits, one of the King, the other of his grandfather King Edward VII, in their costumes as Sovereigns of the Order of the Garter. The King posed for this picture on 8 August 1941. An extract from Sir Owen Morshead's diary indicates the position a year later:

> *16 July 1942* . . . Gerald Kelly is still here but I believe he is due to leave at the end of this month. However I understand that he has been given several more commissions (e.g. a portrait of the King for the Garter Throne Room here) so I expect he may remain. I shall be glad, for I find him an amusing and very intelligent person to have about the house.

Of course, he remained. Morshead's diary provides some justification for the gossip about his Penelope-like methods which Sir Alan Lascelles has noted. Kelly did work over and over again on the velvet and ermine, the gold lace and diamonds of Their Majesties' coronation robes:

> *4 June 1944* . . . Gerald Kelly looked in, as smart as paint in a summer-weight suit of light grey. 'Hullo,' I said, 'you've evidently been down to the Fourth of June?' 'Yes, I have,' he said, 'but with great restraint I painted hard till 4 o'clock, and only then did I allow myself to go down and join the glad throng. And while I was painting a certain passage of the white fur edging to the Queen's robes I suddenly remembered that it was exactly a year ago to the day, the Fourth of June 1943, that I was painting the very same passage in the very same place. I remember it well because that was the day Queen Mary came in and things were going stickily till the dog was sick and everybody loosened up and became merry . . . I wonder how many times I've rubbed *that* bit out and done it again during the past twelve-month?'

Meanwhile, in March 1944, Sir Alfred Munnings had been elected P.R.A. on the death of Sir Edwin Lutyens, defeating Augustus John by 24 votes to 11. Kelly voted for John, and in his letter of congratulation to Munnings, he explained why:

> . . . I did so because I wish above all things to see the rising generation of artists reconciled to the Academy; and I felt that

John was the candidate most likely to bring about this consummation.

You beat him handsomely, and I accept the situation. It is the easier for me to do since for many years I have greatly admired your paintings, and still do so.

I feel certain that we both love this institution, the Royal Academy, and wish to see its traditions honourably maintained . . . In every point that I can, my support, for what little it may be worth, shall be at your service.

In his reply, Munnings said he 'had hoped John would have to bear the burden'. He added: 'You and I will never disagree about things that matter.' It was not an accurate prophecy.

Sir Owen Morshead's diary of 8 March 1945 contains the entry: 'Kenneth Clark came down to vet Gerald's portraits which, believe it or not, are nearly finished and are to be exhibited at the Royal Academy Exhibition.' The State Portraits were duly exhibited at the summer show in 1945, and along with them another portrait that had caused the artist much anxiety, that of J. Craig Harvey. Sir Alfred Munnings described the arrival of the royal portraits in his autobiography:

The artist had been given a week's grace, and the wall at the end of the large gallery was kept for them. We on the Committee welcomed those excellent pictures when they were brought in and hung on the wall.

'Bravo!' said I to Kelly . . . In those large full-length State portraits nothing was shirked . . . I doubt if there is a painter today who would have done those pictures so thoroughly. . . .

The King and Queen, with Princess Elizabeth, and Princess Margaret, were received by Munnings, Kelly, and others when they arrived for a preview of the exhibition on 3 May.

The portraits, wrote the *Times* critic, 'hold the attention . . . Much time has clearly been spent on the accumulation of detail and in giving a high finish and accuracy to the robes and regalia. The same conscientious precision, almost like that of a Dutch painter of still life, is used in the treatment of the clean architectural background and extends to all the simpler parts of the portraits, so that they do not lack that uniformity which many painters fail to get when they bring in minute details.' (*The Times*, 5 May 1945.)

The copying of the State Portraits for the dominions and colonies, and for embassies and legations abroad, occupied many years and gave useful employment, though the delay in finishing the portraits caused, it must be admitted, some frustration and disappointment among potential copyists. The artist fulfilled a long-standing promise when he presented his original sketch for the King's portrait to the British Institute in Florence, of which, as has been said, his cousin was the director.

Kelly had worthily fulfilled his commission and deserved his reward. In July 1945, he was knighted by the King, who hardly knew whether to smile or not when the band played 'Has anybody here seen Kelly?'

The projects for the Garter Throne Room were not pursued; the King's ill-health and untimely death put an end to them. However, a posthumous portrait of the King by Kelly was acquired by the Royal Academy in 1966.

During the war years, Kelly's interests were not confined to Windsor. He was a member of the Royal Fine Art Commission, 1938–43, and when Sir Walter Russell retired from the post of Keeper of the Royal Academy, Kelly took on the job without salary until Philip Connard was appointed in 1945 – it was virtually a sinecure, as the Academy Schools were closed.

An appointment that influenced him profoundly was his selection as Governor of Dulwich College, which dated from 1 December 1944. Under the Act of Parliament controlling the Alleyn Foundation, the President and Council of the Royal Academy are required to nominate one of the Governors, whose special task it is to see that the gallery and its contents are cared for with the best professional advice. From 1945, Kelly became Honorary Surveyor of the Dulwich pictures; he also had to supervise the restoration of Soane's building, seriously damaged by a German bomb. Knowing his great love for the Dulwich gallery since boyhood days in Camberwell, there is no puzzle as to why Kelly volunteered for this task.

4

Sir Owen Morshead's diary yields an item from the early war years at Windsor that deserves quotation:

> 15 August 1940 . . . When someone happened to observe the other day how awful it would be to be known as the husband of the beautiful Mrs So-&-So, Gerald Kelly ejaculated 'Not at all; that's just the position I've been in for the past 20 years, and I assure you it's very gratifying.'

The Kellys' house in Gloucester Place was closed throughout the war, and Jane spent most of it in the country, though she made visits to Windsor. She came there, for instance, when Gerald was ill with amoebic dysentery in 1942. His bedroom was remote; his meals could be taken up, but there was no one to look after him. Jane arrived on a Thursday. By the Sunday morning her husband was a little better, and he told her to put on her best clothes because the Royal Family always lunched with the household on Sundays.

At lunch-time Jane placed herself at the end of the line that awaited the King and Queen, and was told 'Mrs Kelly, come with us.' In the dining-room she was seated next to the King; nearby on the wall hung a picture of Queen Victoria. 'What's that she's got under her feet?' asked the King. 'It's a *pouf*, Sir,' replied Jane. 'But what's it doing there?' asked the King. 'I suppose it's because she was a little woman,' said Jane tentatively.

Years later, when the King came to the Royal Academy, he met Jane again, and soon returned to the subject of Queen Victoria. 'She *was* a little woman,' he said. It was typical of his remarkable memory.

For Jane the year 1944 was notable for her public debut as an artist. Some years earlier, she had cautiously begun to paint a still-life picture. Gerald discovered her doing it and encouraged her to persevere. Now, she decided to try her luck at the Academy.

She was determined to succeed on her own merits, or not at all. It would not do for her to be known as the wife of a prominent R.A. She could not possibly submit her work under her own name, or even from the address in Gloucester Place.

A pseudonym had to be invented. Having started life as Lilian, and later having become not only Jane but also Kelly, she decided on a bizarre combination of all three – Lilian Jelly! And so, in 1944, it was Miss Jelly, giving an obscure address in Chelsea, who had the honour of the acceptance of two paintings in the Royal Academy exhibition: 'Christmas Roses' and 'Lilies of the Valley'.

These were the first of twenty-five still-lifes by the same artist which were accepted by the Academy over the next thirty years. All were admired, and many were sold. Lady Kelly's still-lifes are, in fact, so good that it seems a pity that 'Lilian Jelly' should have been allowed to get away with them.

Kelly's visit to Windsor had been strangely prolonged, but as with other episodes of his career, this one turned out better than might have been expected. Providence, as Kelly put it, was 'constantly interfering on my behalf'.

It was not only that he had triumphed with the State Portraits, after immense labour. He had also spent several years in the Royal Household at a time when the prospects of the Royal Academy were extremely gloomy. The famous exhibition of the King's Pictures at Burlington House in 1946–7 was a direct result of Kelly's stay at Windsor and of the thoughts he had there.

CHAPTER SEVEN

The Great Cleaning Controversy

I

After Kelly had re-opened his house in Gloucester Place at the end of the war he made haste to engage a new secretary. She was Doreen Kennedy, aged 21, just released from the W.R.N.S. When she married, in 1948, Kelly offered with typical generosity to paint her portrait in naval uniform as a wedding present; and he borrowed this picture back from her to show it at the Academy in 1971, the last year of his life, as 'Portrait of a Wren'.

He was delighted to return to his studio. He was habitually cheerful when painting, and used to sing songs from a varied repertory. Dr F. W. Hilles noted one that went:

> *Have you ever heard of Finnigan?*
> *He grew a beard on his chinnigan;*
> *The wind came along and blew't innigan —*
> *Poor old Finnigan. Beginnigan.*

Lady Kelly once went into the studio and found him singing:

> *Postponed my wedding,*
> *Bought a pair of boots instead!*

There were explosive outbursts intermittently. One day Jane heard an altercation coming from the studio while Gerald was painting the official portrait of a distinguished headmistress: she kept asking him how much he was being paid, as she wanted to *buy* the picture. 'Sit down!' Gerald was saying sternly to the headmistress, '*Sit down!*' At which Jane entered innocently to restore calm and harmony.

Jane made herself the perfect wife for a temperamental Irish painter, who was not the easiest person to live with. Gerald realized that she had wisdom. Not only did he love her; he respected her judgement. And he needed this domestic discipline, being naturally impetuous himself. Indeed it is difficult to imagine him making his successful career without Jane's support. She did him nothing but good, and 117 Gloucester Place was a happy house.

2

The Dean of Windsor (Bishop Eric Hamilton), Sir Percy Bates, Dame Caroline Haslett, Sir Malcolm Sargent – who became a close friend – Lady Lewthwaite, Somerset Maugham – now trained as the perfect sitter – and Princess Neslishah, a magnificent Egyptian beauty, were a few of those who, together with Jane, occupied Kelly's attention as a portrait-painter in the years 1945–9. An objective observer may not only marvel at the industry within his studio, but wonder still more at the energy that was left for artistic causes outside. The Royal Academy and the Dulwich Gallery had become principal interests, and Kelly's passionate love of painting involved him increasingly in problems of cleaning and conservation, where he had both the empirical knowledge and the self-confidence to speak his mind.

At the end of the war, an opportunity arose not only to show the public the King's collection of pictures – unknown to most people – but also to benefit the Royal Academy, whose finances, starved through-out the war years, had been helped by grants from the Pilgrim Trust. The exhibition of more than five hundred paintings from the royal col-lections, held at Burlington House in the winter of 1946–7, proved overwhelmingly successful and attracted 366,000 visitors. The income it brought sustained the Academy at a critical time. Sir Alfred Mun-nings wrote about all this with gusto in his autobiography – 'What a noble collection it was, and what a success!' – but it happened that he did not invoke the name of Kelly. Credit can now be given where it is due.

'There is no doubt whatsoever that the idea for the exhibition of the King's Pictures was Kelly's,' writes Sir Anthony Blunt, who was ap-pointed their Surveyor in April 1945. 'He seized what was a unique opportunity because all the pictures in the royal palaces had been taken down and stored during the war and could not be rehung immediately because the palaces themselves needed to be redecorated. He simply went to the King and put the suggestion to him and the King agreed.'

From that point, Blunt was actively involved, for he was the only person in a position to know what could be exhibited. Blunt made the general plans for the exhibition and suggested that the first three rooms should be devoted to portraits (mainly royal), after which the exhibition continued according to schools (Italian, Flemish, and so on). A great deal of the selection was also Blunt's, but Ellis Waterhouse chose the Dutch pictures and helped in many other ways. The selection is attributed in the catalogue to these two, and to Kelly and Benedict Nicolson.

This historic exhibition was managed by a committee of three members of the Royal Academy and three members of the Royal Household, with Sir Ulick Alexander, Keeper of the Privy Purse, as chairman. Kelly and his friend Sir Owen Morshead served on the committee. The following excerpts from Morshead's diary are relevant:

> *25 October 1945* . . . To Buckingham Palace for the first Committee Meeting for next Autumn's big Exhibition . . .
>
> *20 October* 1946 . . . To the pre-view by the Royal Family of the great exhibition in the R.A. A particularly pleasant occasion, with many friends . . .
>
> *6 December* . . . To the Royal Academy to hear Harold Nicolson lecture on the Royal Portraits from the Waterloo Gallery; and on round the Exhibition with Queen Mary and the Princess Royal. Then to an excellent dinner with Gerald & Jane Kelly in their kitchen in Gloucester Place . . .
>
> *18 December* . . . I dined in Town with the Royal Academy who gave a dinner to the Committee of the King's Pictures Exhibition. A delightful Pickwickian evening. Everyone made speeches: Munnings made about seven; I only one, whence I ran for the last train and got back at midnight thoroughly amused – and none the worse for it next day.

The exhibition of the King's Pictures was in every way a happy inspiration. Beyond doubt, Kelly had the financial recuperation of the Academy much more practically in mind than either Lutyens or Munnings, his predecessors as President. Incidentally, the exhibition avoided the necessity of keeping five hundred royal pictures for several further months in West Country and Welsh caves – maintained and staffed at considerable cost – until their proper homes could be refurnished to receive them once more.

3

In the nineteen-thirties two German refugees, both expert in the conservation and restoration of paintings, settled in England. They were Helmut Ruhemann (1891–1973) and Dr Johann Hell (1897–1974).

Ruhemann became associated with the radical cleaning policy adopted at the National Gallery after the appointment of Sir Philip Hendy as its Director in 1946. Hendy believed strongly in scientific methods, reacted passionately against the retention of discoloured varnishes, and went about as far as anyone with his responsibilities could do in encouraging Ruhemann to clean the pictures down to the original paint. His eye being accustomed to the bold if not blatant colouring of his favourite painter Matthew Smith, Hendy had no objection to the Old Masters looking as if they had been painted yesterday morning under an arc light.

Dr Hell had different ideas. He had been a pupil in Berlin of Oskar Fischel,* the great German art-historian and authority on Raphael, and like him was gentle, friendly, and modest. He was a craftsman of subtle aesthetic and artistic sensibility who worked slowly and believed that a picture-cleaner owed his chief duty to art rather than science. He made his way rapidly in England with the support of such eminent art experts as Paul Oppé.

What Gerald Kelly and others like Oppé chiefly complained about was that the Old Masters were never intended to look like Matthew Smiths. And here they were undoubtedly right. 'The trouble was,' writes Benedict Nicolson, 'that nobody really knew what they *ought* to look like, and so an alternative solution was never discoverable, except to the extent that it was sensible to maintain that it was preferable in some cases to retain some repaint, dirt, or varnish over very badly damaged areas, because the half-truth that resulted therefrom was preferable to the lie that the revelation of old damages, discolourations, etc., caused.' Dr Hell followed this principle, and, if he erred, it was on the side of caution.

* Dr Fischel, who was married to a distant cousin of mine, followed his pupil to England in 1939, but, sadly, did not live long in exile. I was present at their joyful reunion, which appropriately took place in the room containing the Raphael Cartoons at the Victoria and Albert Museum. D.H.

4

When Kelly was appointed Honorary Surveyor of the Dulwich Gallery in 1945, the Dulwich pictures were stored in the vaults of the National Library of Wales, Aberystwyth. Having met Johann Hell at Windsor (where he cleaned many of the royal pictures), Kelly soon decided to entrust the Dulwich Collection to his care. Kelly and Dr Hell together visited Aberystwyth, where they found the pictures badly in need of attention. They drew up a plan of action, based on a strict order of priority. The work of cleaning and restoring began almost immediately at Dr Hell's Hampstead studio, while the repairing and partial rebuilding of the Dulwich Gallery after its bomb damage went on at the same time.

Kelly's love of the place increased the more he had to do with it. For him Dulwich was a gallery large enough to hold many masterpieces, from Rubens and Rembrandt to Watteau and Gainsborough, yet small enough to retain that intimacy in which a visitor could feel alone with them individually. Kelly's enthusiasm fired others to work for Dulwich. His own energy and perseverance were, however, essential, for it was not until 1953 that the building (restored with the generous help of the Pilgrim Trust) and the pictures (restored by Dr Hell's slow and careful craftsmanship) were ready for their triumphant re-opening.

Meanwhile it was not surprising that Kelly's friendship with Dr Hell, combined with his responsibilities at Dulwich and his lifelong preoccupation with painting techniques, should have made him think about problems of conservation and restoration in general. There had already been some discussion during Kenneth Clark's directorship over the cleaning of Velasquez's full-length portrait of Philip IV at the National Gallery; Lord Clark believes himself that the legs became too white and that 'the restorer had taken off the last film of varnish when I was out at lunch'. But this particular picture has recovered itself, and the controversy about it was nothing compared with the explosion which followed publication of a letter in *The Times* of 30 October 1946:

Sir, I believe that a series of terrible mistakes has occurred in the National Gallery. Some pictures – alas, they were masterpieces – have been so drastically cleaned that worn and spoiled passages in them are only too visible. Assuming that all the damage in these pictures, now revealed to our disillusioned eyes, was done in the past, surely it is unwise to spoil the unity of an old picture just to lay bare the ruined state of the original? It is profoundly regrettable that so satisfactory a picture as the great Koninck landscape should have been reduced to an incoherent ruin. The renewal of the policy of extreme cleaning, as revealed, for example, in the 'Chapeau de Paille' by Rubens and the 'Woman Bathing' by Rembrandt, seems likely to produce a fresh crop of unfortunate results.

I am informed that there are other pictures that have been cleaned but not yet exhibited. The process is going on. The empty frame of Philip IV,* 'removed for examination', fills me with terror and foreboding. Surely the safety of the national treasures should take precedence over every other consideration?

I appeal to the trustees (i) to call a halt to this dangerous activity; (ii) to exhibit in one group all the pictures that have been cleaned and restored during the last 10 years, so that what has been done may be exactly estimated.

It is well known that most old paintings have suffered through age, decay, and restorers. Though it is desirable to remove disfiguring brown varnish, it is possible to stop before removing all of it. (It is during the removal of the last vestiges of the old varnish from the impasto that fresh damage is done.) A very thin layer of the old varnish, even though discoloured, does not really interfere with the appearance of a picture in the pitiless light of the modern gallery for which no pictures were ever made. And, furthermore, this thin layer will protect the surface of the picture when next it comes to be cleaned; for let us remember that any new varnish now put on will inevitably discolour, become opaque, and call for removal.

I do not denounce the cleaning of pictures. Tenderly done it can have admirable results. The portraits of Mme Moitessier and of M. de Norvins by Ingres, Antonello's 'San Jerome', the big Caravaggio, the 'Christ at Emmaus', and 'The Cleansing of the Temple' by El Greco have greatly benefited and look magnificent. But, alas, this cannot be said for Rubens's great 'War and Peace'.

I should like the trustees to remember that during the seventies of the last century cathedrals and churches of this country were ruthlessly restored, and we still bewail the harm done by the well-meaning men who were entrusted with the work. With what

* The bust portrait of Philip IV when elderly.

disillusioned eyes will a future generation regard the pictures we loved when they are confronted with the unfortunate results of the activities of the cleaners and restorers of today!

Yours, etc.,

GERALD KELLY.

Kelly was supported in *The Times* by letters from Rodrigo Moynihan, Anthony Devas, Sir Alfred Munnings, Thomas Bodkin, Henry Lamb, Leonard Greaves, Maurice Brockwell, Allan Gwynne-Jones, Paul Oppé, and Dame Laura Knight. On the other side there were letters from Victor Pasmore and Albert Houthuesen, and a letter from Clive Bell and others maintaining that sometimes a risk must be taken in cleaning. A leading article on 3 December summed up the correspondence; it was non-committal, but inclined, if anything, to favour Kelly's point of view. On 7 December, *The Times* published another letter from Kelly:

> Sir, In your leading article of December 3, you summarize the arguments which have been put forward on the subject of cleaning pictures by the various correspondents in *The Times*. In the last paragraph of the article there is one point which, I feel, needs comment. The issue is not, as implied there, between those who support cleaning and those who oppose it; it is between two different methods of cleaning. No reasonable person can doubt that pictures must of necessity be cleaned; the problem is, how should they be cleaned?
>
> The alternatives are not, therefore, cleaning and no cleaning, but rather the use, on the one hand, of a method which appears to involve unnecessary risks, or, on the other, of one which gives the greatest security against damage and leaves at every stage an opportunity of stopping the process at the wisest moment. The method I believe in has only one disadvantage – it is extremely slow. Is there such a hurry? Are not these pictures of great value? Is not damage to a picture irretrievable?
>
> Yours faithfully,
>
> GERALD KELLY.

This was Kelly's last shot in the skirmish. In the sporadic correspondence that continued, *The Times* published letters in his support from Augustus John, T. J. Honeyman, Director of Glasgow Art Gallery, and Francis Howard; letters in favour of the National Gallery were contributed by the distinguished octogenarian scientist Dr A. P. Laurie, who had specialized in the study of painting materials. At about the beginning of 1947 a petition for an inquiry into the whole matter was presented to the Prime Minister by sixty artists (of whom Kelly was not one). As a result, an exhibition of the pictures cleaned by the National Gallery since 1936 was announced for the autumn, and a three-man committee was appointed by the Gallery to investigate the complaints.

Part of Kelly's appeal to the Trustees had therefore been met; but his request that they should 'call a halt to this dangerous activity' was either ignored or made too late so far as Velasquez's small portrait of Philip IV was concerned. After the cleaned Velasquez had been replaced in the gallery in the Spring of 1947, *The Times* was bombarded with more letters of protest. Kelly kept silent, but Sir Alfred Munnings declared that the head was 'utterly and irretrievably ruined' (3 May), Neville Lytton agreed (6 May), and a further group of twenty Royal Academicians, though not Kelly, supported the proposition that 'the small portrait of Philip IV . . . is no longer a great work of art' (7 May). Francis Dodd wrote in the opposite sense (12 May), but on 15 May Oswald Birley pronounced that the portrait had been 'ruined for all time' and Thomas Bodkin that there had been an 'irremediable disaster'.

The National Gallery was entitled to its hour of satisfaction when the promised display of the cleaned pictures was mounted. About thirty distinguished figures in the art world then wrote to *The Times* to express approval of what had been done (18 October). Readers of *The Times* had to wait a further six months (8 May 1948) for an article by Dr J. R. H. Weaver, President of Trinity College, Oxford, the chairman of the committee of inquiry, who felt able to state that the pictures most often complained about had not been damaged and were 'in first-rate condition'. And thus the curtain fell on the combatants, with W. G. de Glehn, R.A., asserting that the report took no account of how the pictures looked and that Philip IV had 'disappeared for ever' (12 May), and with Thomas Bodkin still indignant (18 May).

5

Was Kelly's effort unnecessarily alarmist, and was it a failure? The answer is No to both questions. Kelly had been justified in sounding an urgent warning; his letters and the support they evoked had a considerable effect on art-gallery directors throughout the British Isles, influencing them towards moderation in their cleaning policies.

There may be some truth in the theory that the controversy revolved around matters of taste – what people thought the Old Masters ought to look like. But there was more to it than that. It is better to be safe than sorry. Kelly found himself in the position of a loving and responsible householder who saw his favourite rose-trees being excessively pruned and likely to fail. After the formal vindication of the National Gallery, he must have been reminded of the old comment 'Operation successful – patient died.'

'I remember well Kelly's intervention on the cleaning of the Rubens "Chapeau de Paille" and "Philip IV when Old",' writes Lord Clark (1973), 'and I was in fact on his side. I think that both pictures have now settled down, but the Philip has never quite recovered its old mystery. I also agreed with Kelly that on the whole Hell was a safer restorer than Ruhemann, but Ruhemann was a teacher, and it was owing to his influence that the National Gallery founded its present admirable scientific department.'

This may be a suitably ambiguous note on which to leave an argument that will never attain finality. The present writer is, however, delighted to know that many of the best pictures in England have been cleaned by Dr Johann Hell.

6

It was during the Great Cleaning Controversy that I personally became aware of Kelly as an original character rather than a conventional exhibitor at the Royal Academy shows. In 1946–7 I was, in fact, sitting in *The Times* office, dealing with the letters he and his friends and opponents were sending to the Editor about the proceedings at the National Gallery. In the Spring of 1948, I asked his advice about my book on James Pryde, and was greatly impressed by the enormous trouble he took to help, writing me four letters in as many weeks. I was then living with my wife and small daughter in a flat on the edge of Battersea Park, and at my suggestion he and Lady Kelly took tea with us, one day in June, and visited the L.C.C. exhibition of statues in the Park. I remember Kelly pausing before one of Maillol's nudes, and mentioning that he had known the sculptor. In front of one or two pieces by Henry Moore he said very little.

What should be said about modern art by Royal Academicians was a question much on Kelly's mind in those years. His cosmopolitan values and intellectual awareness separated him sharply from the then President, the ultra-English extrovert Sir Alfred Munnings. It was not that he failed to appreciate Munnings' good qualities as a painter or a man – rather that he was urgently aware of the dangers lurking for the Royal Academy in Munnings' arrogant campaign against modern art in general.

For two of Munnings' initiatives, Kelly had every sympathy – the election of Sir Winston Churchill as Royal Academician Extraordinary in 1948, and the exhibition in 1949 of all the pictures acquired by the Chantrey Bequest. But a warning he conveyed to Munnings shows how much he objected to being taken for granted and caught up in the whirlwind of the latter's brash assumptions:

> 8 February 1949.
>
> My dear A.J. Oh, how I wish you hadn't this appetite for publicity. I'm shocked at your 'bustling catchpenny tactics'. Alas, alas! I received the copy of *Picture Post* sent with somebody's compliments. Oh! horrible, you were at it again and worse. The same sincerity which is so lovable – yes, but you mention living artists and members of our body. It's not fair. You shouldn't do it. It makes so many of us ashamed. How difficult it is to write, to paint, to criticize and to collect well and wisely!
>
> Yours ever,
>
> GERALD KELLY.

Unfortunately, Kelly's warning was not heeded. When the Royal Academy banquet was revived in 1949, at Churchill's suggestion, after a lapse of ten years, Munnings made an incoherent Blimp-ish speech against modern art, which perhaps by its unexpectedness created an even more startling impression on those who heard it over the radio – it was broadcast while heavy rain rattled on the gallery roof – than it did on those who were actually present at Burlington House (and that is saying something!). His speech included references to 'affected juggling' and 'damned nonsense'; a gratuitous attack on one of his guests, Anthony Blunt, for admiring Picasso; and an onslaught on the sculpture exhibition in Battersea Park – 'we are spending millions every year on art education, and still we exhibit all these foolish drolleries to the public'.

Munnings was later rebuked by Churchill for involving him in a derogatory reference to Picasso in the speech. It was true that Churchill was no friend of modern art, but the President offended him by giving publicity to a private joke between them, and Munnings admitted 'Maybe I did go too far.'

The naïvety of the speech pleased many, but left an appalling impression on intelligent listeners of the incapacity of the Royal Academy to initiate artistic reconciliation or constructive leadership. Munnings knew this would be his only speech at an Academy banquet. He answered interruptions by saying: 'As I am President and have the right of the Chair, allow me to speak. I shall not be here next year, thank God!'

It was to be left to Kelly to try to heal some of the wounds left by that disastrous evening. It fell to him also to have the last word on the subject in his article on Munnings in the *Dictionary of National Biography*:

> Unfortunately he chose the occasion to make a prejudiced, indiscreet speech in which he spoke ill of artists of whom he disapproved and of modern art in general. His hostility towards the whole modern movement made him unable to believe that any sincere artist could think differently from himself.

The Kelly temperament was well displayed at 117 Gloucester Place on 8 December 1949. Kelly's secretary had forgotten to remind him of an important meeting to be held at the Academy that day to elect a new President. There was general confusion in the house.

Kelly's temper erupted. 'Anyway, do you think I want to be President of the Royal Academy and do all those dreadful chores?' he asked Jane with most unusual ferocity, gripping her arm.

'Well, all right then, you don't,' said Jane very quietly, 'so why fuss about it?'

Kelly put on his hat and overcoat and picked up his umbrella. He was soon his usual brisk self again.

At the front door he turned and looked back. 'Wish me luck!' he said.

CHAPTER EIGHT

The President

'One thing is certain, he is about the best president the Royal Academy has given itself since Sir Joshua Reynolds. He has raised that foundation from the depths of public contempt to respectability if not honour.'

Clive Bell on Sir Gerald Kelly in *Old Friends*, 1956.

I

Kelly was elected President on 8 December 1949, with a majority over R. G. Brundrit in the second ballot of twenty votes to thirteen. He was seventy but had the vitality of a man much younger. During the next decade he made himself one of the best-known figures in England, communicating his zest for painting and his lively humanity to millions who heard him on the radio or saw him on television. Yet the fame that came to Kelly as P.R.A., and as the first great popularizer of the visual arts in the new medium, was incidental to his one great object, the revival of the fortunes of his beloved Royal Academy. A new broom was urgently needed there; expenses increased daily; the value of money had declined; the rantings broadcast by Munnings had lowered the Academy's esteem in the art world even among those who were disposed to be friendly.

'No two men ever had the same opinion about art,' said Kelly after his election, in reply to a question about the future of art (*The Times*, 9 December). 'I think that modern art, like every other art, has in it some good, some bad, and some indifferent, and some of it is danged bad.'

The pronouncement was not intended to be revolutionary, yet it marked an advance on the attitude of Sir Alfred Munnings. If an element of cantankerousness remained, it was more discriminatingly applied.

Mrs Harrison, 1907
(oil, 68″ × 29½″).

Elizabeth Heygate,
oil, 1909
(*see* pp. 34–5).

Ma Si Gyaw IV, 1909, sold for a gift to Tate Gallery (oil, 50″ × 40″).

The Jester (W. Somerset Maugham), 1911 (oil, 40″ × 30″).

Queen Elizabeth,
the State Portrait
(oil, 107″ × 70″).

Jane XXX, 1930,
Diploma work
(oil, 29½″ × 24½″).

The Academy no longer had a President of the extreme right, but one who stood much nearer to the centre. Out walking in the street, with his black hat, Old Etonian tie, and rolled umbrella, Kelly might appear the embodiment of English tradition. The impression was misleading. The years spent in France, Spain, and Burma, and his travels around the world, had left him with broad cosmopolitan views, and a deep knowledge and sympathetic understanding of art and artists everywhere. A love of poetry was implicit in his adult character, Pope and Browning being among his favourite poets. Such a background was unlikely to produce an insular President. And in Kelly's case, his essential Irishness had always made him see the English with something of a foreigner's detachment.

His own verdict on the Irish, as recorded in Dr F. W. Hilles's diary (5 January 1931), was nevertheless severe. 'A rotten race ethnographically speaking,' Kelly had said, 'they aren't far from the monkey.' Dr Hilles noted that Kelly's sympathies in the Anglo-Irish disputes seemed to be with the English; but Kelly had emphasized 'My favourite race is the Spanish.'

Kelly now became the first Irish President since Sir Martin Archer Shee (1830–50), and was accorded an honorary LL.D. at Trinity College, Dublin. He received the same honour from Cambridge University, but perhaps another distinction pleased him more than any: 'Remember to put down that I'm the only Old Etonian ever to become P.R.A.,' he told Dennis Farr when the latter was compiling the Tate Gallery Catalogue of the Modern British School, published 1964–5; 'Now that's a record worth quoting and says something about our Public Schools, too!' ('Sadly, we did not record this in quite the way he wished,' adds Mr Farr.)

Somerset Maugham's letter of congratulation was dated 8 December, the day of Kelly's election:

> I write this in the hope that my letter will be the first to reach you addressed P.R.A.
> I need not tell you how thrilled & excited I was to hear the good news.
> Do you remember Paris in 1904? We did not imagine then that either of us would come to the point we have. . . .

He could not resist one of his avuncular admonitions:

> Finally, I hope you will be as urbane and as tolerant of other people's stupidity in your new position as your irascible temper

will permit. After all you have to make up for your predecessor's mistakes if you want to maintain the dignity of the institution.

As for that unrepentant predecessor, Sir Alfred Munnings, he was delighted to have got away. He was soon writing to Kelly (20 December 1949): 'Here is a letter for the P.R.A. I send it on to you & I am sure in your new position, full of fervour, you will not let it go unheeded!' He concluded with a drawing of a dancing figure labelled 'The freedom loving P.P.R.A.'

2

At first, Munnings was pleased to think of Kelly as his successor, but rapidly he became disillusioned in him. Of course he accepted that Kelly was an admirer of Augustus John, and that Kelly would do all he could to retain John's interest in the Royal Academy (John having already resigned once as R.A. and been reinstated in 1940). But when Kelly made it his immediate business to secure the reinstatement as a full Academician of Stanley Spencer* – which he achieved at a General Assembly of the Academy on 17 January 1950 – Munnings was moved to grumble. Kelly told him on 23 January: 'I don't think Spencer will do the Academy any harm. He is almost uncannily skilful and a lovely craftsman.' After the Chantrey Bequest had bought one of Spencer's pictures, with Kelly's encouragement, in May 1950, Munnings' dislike of Spencer and his work was renewed; he called the figures in the picture 'barrel-like human beings, stark, pseudo-comic; hands like bunches of bananas'.

There was worse to come. Munnings discovered that Spencer had painted certain canvases that might be termed pornographic. He obtained photographs of these pictures which he showed indignantly to the Dean of Westminster and to a police inspector at Newmarket! – hoping presumably that retribution of some sort would follow. Nothing happened, except that the Council of the Royal Academy recorded their sympathy with Spencer in his harassment, and Kelly reluctantly accused Munnings of 'caddishness' in that he might have brought the Academy into disrepute. Charitable observers would probably agree that these disturbing erotic works of Spencer's reflect the psycho-

* Spencer had resigned as A.R.A. in 1935, after two of his pictures had been rejected by the Hanging Committee.

logical tensions of an imaginative painter rather than anything more sinister.*

Kelly managed to smooth over the disturbance. It was largely owing to him that Spencer, who was made C.B.E. in 1950 and knighted in 1959, received official recognition of his genius. Spencer wrote to him from Cookham Rise on 14 November 1950:

> Dear Sir Gerald Kelly,
>
> Thank you for your kind letter. It was very kind of you to do what you did for me. I would like to meet you again & I could see you any time you appointed at the R.A., Piccadilly.
>
> Yours sincerely,
STANLEY SPENCER.
>
> P.S. I agree that nothing can be done in the matter of which you write, but I could not say myself that I had 'received no material damage'.

3

Generous space was given to Spencer's work at the summer exhibition of 1950, and he was present as a full R.A. at the first annual dinner of Kelly's presidency on 27 April 1950. Kelly chose an austere menu to emphasize the Academy's financial straits, and they sat down to lobster patties, cold roast ribs of beef and Stilton cheese, backed up by burgundy, claret and port. The Academy's principal guests were Clement Attlee (the Prime Minister), Sir John Slessor, Douglas Clifton Brown (Speaker of the House of Commons), Robert Birley (Head Master of Eton), and Winston Churchill. Proposing the health of the guests, Kelly described them as 'a noble group of, oh, how distinguished men, all hand-picked'. There was laughter when he added 'and I took a lot of trouble'.

It was a successful dinner but fraught with complications behind the scenes, as Sir Robert Birley explains.

> I became Head Master of Eton in September, 1949 [writes Sir Robert Birley]. Sir Gerald was the first Etonian to be President. I think that was why he invited me to the Banquet and to reply for the Guests.

* I am grateful to the present owner for showing me a photograph of one of the contentious pictures. D.H.

Then a very odd difficulty arose. Various people make speeches after the President, such as the Prime Minister, before the person who replies for the Guests. On this occasion, Sir Gerald invited Winston Churchill to speak after me, an additional speech. The B.B.C. very badly wanted to give Churchill's speech, but in order to do this (as a result of some problem of timing) they decided *not* to have Attlee's speech as Prime Minister. On this, Attlee said that he would not speak. This would have been an appalling breach with tradition. Sir Gerald got on to the B.B.C. and they agreed to include both. But, again because of some problem of timing, it was necessary to keep things going for longer than had been allowed for before Churchill spoke.

Sir Gerald got in touch with me and asked me if I would be ready to speak for twenty minutes instead of for ten. Of course I had to say that I would. It was no mean task. How I kept it going I don't know. I must have been intolerably boring. I remember getting two days later a letter signed by three young men from the East India Club just saying, approximately, this, 'For God's sake shut up and sit down. We cannot stand it any longer.' The *Sketch* (or it may have been the *Tatler*) had a piece referring to how intolerably long-winded I had been.

I did not see this, but Sir Gerald got to hear of it and wrote them a letter, which they published I think, explaining why it was I had spoken for so long. Someone told me of this and I felt extremely grateful to him. It was just like him to do this.

I wonder if I may add an account of two incidents at that dinner involving Winston Churchill. I have always greatly treasured them.

One of the toasts at the dinner is to His (Her) Majesty's Government. At the dinner I was sitting on Sir Gerald's left, Attlee on his right. Winston Churchill sat on my left. When the toast was proposed Churchill left his seat, shuffled along behind myself and Sir Gerald, came up behind Attlee, got him to turn round, raised his glass and said, 'Clem, my dear fellow, on this neutral ground, may I drink your health.'

I had just done nearly three years work in Germany dealing with German education and I had often quoted to German politicians Lord Haldane's deeply significant remark, 'Parliamentary democracy is only possible when the Government meets the Opposition out to dinner.' I remember wishing that some of them had been there. Since then, when speaking in Germany, I have often used that incident.

The second incident came later, after the dinner. I was moving across the hall when I saw that Winston Churchill and the Archbishop of Canterbury (Fisher) were having an argument. The Archbishop, with his back to the wall, was clearly on the defensive. I came up to listen. The argument was about the Revised Edition of Hymns Ancient and Modern, which had just come out. 'But it's perfectly all right,' the Archbishop said. 'You'll find all those old hymns you like are still in the new edition. The only thing changed will be their numbers.' To which Churchill replied, 'Yes, but we like the old numbers'.

In his tribute at the dinner to his predecessor Sir Alfred Munnings, Kelly tactfully said 'he caused either delightful anticipation or fearful qualms, according to the dovecote in which he proposed to flutter'. Offering his own olive branch to the modern movement, he announced that the Academy proposed to hold a small exhibition 'of more or less contemporary European pictures which would include the best examples of modern art they could find'. Kelly 'hoped that all students of art would see them, as the exhibition was designed both to help and to warn'. In May he went over to Paris with Edward Le Bas to make arrangements for this exhibition, which emerged in January 1951, as L'École de Paris, 1900–1950.

He wrote to Robert Birley (12 May 1950) accepting his invitation to visit Eton for the Fourth of June celebrations: 'I should like to come down for Speeches very much, and I adore fireworks! Jane will come with me so that I know I shall enjoy it.' In the same letter he petitioned the headmaster, unsuccessfully, for a whole holiday for the school to celebrate his election as President.*

A serious disappointment of 1950 was the breakdown of negotiations for an exhibition of German art, which had been an ambition of the Royal Academy since Ribbentrop frustrated an earlier project in 1938. In the short space of three months, Kelly had to supervise the organization of a substitute exhibition of Works by Holbein and Other Masters of the 16th and 17th Centuries which opened in December. It was not achieved without stress or some frayed tempers among his advisers. Kelly himself wrote to many of the lenders, and took endless pains to show a personal interest. But once again, the Academy was saved by the King's gracious offer of support, more than half the 450 exhibits coming from the royal collection. Kelly had always been a loyal subject of the Crown; as P.R.A., his patriotism glowed.

* See p. 7.

4

Pamela Mansel became Kelly's secretary in May 1950, and was with him throughout the trials of his presidency until she left to become Mrs McClintock in July 1953.

The three years I worked for him were terrifying, gay, exhausting, thrilling, impossible, interesting, full, alive – but above all *worth while* [writes Mrs McClintock]. Accepted as one of the family from the moment of your arrival, and expected to accept the Kellys' standards, you had to be utterly loyal, to work for a pittance (and until the work was finished), you had somehow to make Sir Gerald cope with the letter-writing connected with administrative work which he had taken on for the Royal Academy and also with his work as Honorary Surveyor of the Dulwich College Picture Gallery. Of course I did not know him before he was P.R.A., but I believe he used to paint practically every day until the light failed. When he was elected president and started to plan the big Winter Exhibitions and the exhibitions to be held in the refurbished Diploma Gallery, his painting time was drastically cut down, so much so that although he had the right to have six paintings hung in the Summer Exhibitions, he never had painted six in the year to send. As President he sat on many more Committees and he insisted on writing personal letters to ask for the loan of pictures for the R.A. Exhibitions. What a time it all took, and this on top of his normal correspondence and the correspondence to do with his Enthusiasms!

There always seemed to be an Enthusiasm on the go – collecting and listing Japanese prints sent from Japan by friends, ordering special hams from America, buying up murder stories by some American authors, finding special blue hydrangeas and painting them, reorganizing his library (which we did all wrong and he was very cross and used it as a goad for years), getting special colours from Robersons and grinding and mixing them himself, listing and indexing his collection of frames, searching for Gadelan tulips (I had to go to Chelsea Flower Show personally and collect some for him), preparing his own canvases, tracking down Real Captain's Biscuits (that was a long one), all of such vital and all-excluding importance while the seizure lasted and so exasperating for his secretary when letters one felt to be more important were pushed aside and forgotten (even hidden if one became too persistent), and yet somehow in the end one always found Sir Gerald Knew Best.

You also had to arrange sittings for the various portraits being painted and to get Sir Gerald to the studio on time – with the right portrait on the easel at the moment that the sitter arrived. This was difficult, for it seemed to me Sir Gerald woke each morning and planned a lovely day for himself of painting or pottering with never a thought to letter-writing or administrative work or of a special portrait to be painted. Just a lovely day of walking into his studio and painting whatever he felt like! As he ran downstairs to his breakfast, the sight of his secretary standing at the bottom with a basket of letters and list of engagements for the day was never a very happy one. Worse still would be the sight of his hat, wallet, money, scarf, keys, arm-length cuffs for buttoning on to his short-sleeved shirts (his own invention I believe, very useful for artists), and umbrella laid out tidily on the hall table ready for him to leave to attend a meeting away from 117 and his studio.

Sir Gerald was short, dapper, and with the most unruly hair in the world. To control it he wore a special sort of hair net under his painting hat which was a wide crownless brim of very light olive green material. For painting he wore a boilersuit of pale blue cotton over his clothes. *How* I should love to see him again in full painting kit step backwards from the easel so that he could peer over his glasses up the shallow studio steps and along the hall to find out who was coming in at the front door – for it must be admitted he had the most insatiable curiosity of anyone I knew and liked to know exactly what was going on in the rest of the house. Even the arrival of the laundry (Thursday lunchtimes I think) was an event to be savoured. Of course, quite often it was the sitter he had already forgotten about, and then there was a busy moving round of easels and wheeling forward of the portrait he should have been working on while I held back the sitter as long as I could with fatuous conversation.

Being Sir Gerald he was able to bring out the interesting side of even the dull sitters and such was his charm and curiosity and conversation that I think all sitters enjoyed their sittings and so, I think, did Sir Gerald once he realized that he had to abandon his happy plans for the day.

Sir Gerald was often invited to speak at public dinners; at first he enjoyed doing this, but he put so much time into writing a good speech that it interfered with his work and eventually Lady Kelly put her foot down. But whilst the speech-making period was on it was very hard work for us all. I remember especially a speech prepared for the Worshipful Company of Fanmakers and G.F.K. writing and rewriting it with only one constant phrase – a description of Spanish girls playing with their fans . . . 'flick, flick, flick'. After Sir Gerald had finally polished a speech to his own satisfaction (and that's saying something!) I had to write it all out in words almost half an inch tall on sheets of halfquarto paper, five lines to a page. These had to be bound together with treasury tags and each bottom left-hand corner turned up individually so that they would be easy to turn. Once Sir Gerald came trotting down the stairs the morning after making a five-minute speech (which had taken us some three days of hard unhappy labour to write): 'I can get rid of you at last! The Prime Minister and the Archbishop of Canterbury have both offered you a job! Jane! Miss Mansel's going and I'll be able to do some painting without her bullying me.' Apparently he had been sitting between Dr Fisher and Mr Churchill when he made his speech and they enjoyed watching him speaking so easily and both felt someone writing out their sermons and parliamentary speeches in the same way would ease their paths.

The more I write of him the more the whole happy concentrated atmosphere of 117 comes back. And yet I have hardly mentioned Lady Kelly who was the loved centre of all our lives. But that is as it should be, for a more quiet self-effacing person would be hard to imagine, and yet she was absolutely essential to us all. She ran 117, Sir Gerald, the studio, everything, with a quiet peaceful patient and humorous efficiency which is hard to describe. Without her in the house, Sir Gerald collapsed, was restless, cross and dis-spirited; with her there, he could relax or survive the most crashing disappointments. And I knew that I could always go to Lady Kelly for support in a crisis, for at Gloucester Place you felt you were one of a team of three and were needed. Even the keeping of five engagement diaries was worth it: one was the Master diary, one was Lady Kelly's, one was the day's event sheet kept on the hall table, one was Sir Gerald's pocket diary, and the last was Sir Gerald's second pocket diary for when he lost the first!

After I left to get married I asked him to give me a reference, and again at various moments I asked him to vouch for me. What a wonderfully staunch friend he was – and what fun!

Sir Gerald, although very careful with small sums of money, was very generous. He contributed half the cost of a mechanized bicycle I had set my heart on, and then lent me his padded boiler suit when I found how cold fast bicycling was (and waved me off!).

Another time, when the King and Queen were attending a R.A. Soirée (I think the King was there, but I'm not sure), he told me I must be around to be presented. 'I'm not going, Sir Gerald.' 'Not going? Of course you are.' I told him I couldn't; I had nothing to wear. Looking rather startled, he left the room, and a few minutes later Lady Kelly appeared and said 'Gerald says I'm to take you out and buy you a dress for tonight.' It was just like them both, and so was the final touch as Sir Gerald came to the door with us and said 'Don't be long, the telephone might ring!'

CHAPTER NINE

Exhibitions at Burlington House

I

Having made an immediate gesture towards healing the breach between the Academy and artists outside, by obtaining the re-election of Stanley Spencer, Kelly next turned his attention to the Academy's finances. If he thought it salutary to introduce a note of austerity into its hospitality, he took care to install an internal telephone to promote efficiency. He also reorganized the Academy's investments, establishing an expert financial advisory committee. His chief effort was, however, directed towards procuring a great increase in the number of exhibitions presented at Burlington House.

Realizing that the public had been starved of pictures throughout the war, and that a new generation had been brought up on reproductions, Kelly was determined to see the Academy fulfil its educational role, and perhaps make a little necessary profit as well. He therefore insisted on a full annual programme for the main galleries, but decided to use the Diploma Gallery, on the top floor, as an additional area for exhibitions. Seven of the loan exhibitions during his presidency, 1949–54, were seen altogether by over one million visitors – these were *Holbein and other Masters*, *The First Hundred Years of the Royal Academy*, *Leonardo Quincentenary*, *Dutch Pictures*, *Kings and Queens*, *Flemish Art*, and *European Masters of the Eighteenth Century*.

Humphrey Brooke, who succeeded Sir Walter Lamb as Secretary of the Academy in 1952, has emphasized Kelly's individual responsibility for these exhibitions (*The Times*, 11 January 1972):

> It was part of Kelly's flair that they were organized on a personal basis – naturally with the best advice – so all profits accrued directly to the Royal Academy. This was a new procedure to that

in force during the big loan exhibitions of the 1930s. Kelly was also responsible for converting the Diploma Gallery into an additional site for exhibitions, of which the Leonardo alone had an attendance of 213,000, more than had visited the gallery in its history.

The correspondence files of the Academy indicate how hard Kelly worked in 1951 to get the Diploma Gallery opened. The change of policy meant that these rooms could not be used for their primary purpose of displaying the diploma works deposited by R.A.s. But economic necessity was overriding. Kelly told Sir Ulick Alexander, Keeper of the Privy Purse, that the Academy had to earn another £3,000 a year (12 April 1951). He continued his letter:

> There is only one way in which we could do it, and that is by using the old 'Diploma Gallery' for smallish exhibitions of great quality. The Gallery was dismantled in 1939, was damaged, and we have only just got to the end of reconditioning it. It has four magnificent rooms, splendidly lit, at the top of seventy stony stairs. It used to be one of the most discreet meeting places for lovers, for they were young and could skip up the stairs and, once there, were free from interruption because they could hear the steps of anyone approaching.

The last sentence – typical of that twinkling humanity which made Kelly such an appealing writer and speaker – had been introduced to emphasize that the Academy's plans might be foiled; there was a danger that a lift could not be installed before the opening of the Leonardo da Vinci Quincentenary Exhibition in March 1952. He wondered whether a hint from Buckingham Palace might persuade Messrs Waygood-Otis to get a move on.

So important did that lift become, in Kelly's mind, to the solvency of the Royal Academy, that he could not resist playing his trump card. He brought the lift into his speech at the annual dinner of 2 May 1951, broadcast by the B.B.C.:

> . . . The Diploma Gallery, my Lords and Gentlemen, which some of you may have heard of – a few of you may even have visited it – is up 70 stone steps and, as your Excellencies and your Graces may know, in this degenerate age people have lost the habit of walking upstairs. We have therefore to put in a lift . . . It is not from the Ministry of Works that I fear difficulty . . . We are

prepared to pay for it. Our hopes, our aspirations, our plans are
all at the mercy of Mr Waygood or Mr Otis or both.

It will come as no surprise, after this, that the lift was ready in time
for the Leonardo Exhibition.

The Prime Minister (Attlee), Admiral Lord Cork and Orrery, Lord
Samuel, and Winston Churchill were other speakers at that dinner, but
the limelight was stolen by Somerset Maugham. Responding to his old
friend the President's proposal of the toast of literature, Maugham reported an imaginary conversation with an elderly lady in tweeds who
had come up from Cheltenham to 'do' the Academy – one of those
ladies who doesn't pretend to know anything about art 'but knows
what she likes'. In preparing this amusing speech, which he delivered
with characteristic hesitant charm, Maugham had obviously taken great
pains. It could almost be called a lesson in friendship.

Maugham had always thought that Kelly would make a good President, and now in his letters to him he more than once congratulated
himself on his prescience.

2

The new broom wielded by Kelly brusquely interrupted the time-
honoured procedures of the Academy, which he described as a 'stately
minuet'. Before he became president, requests for the lending of
pictures had tended to be formal and stereotyped. Kelly's individual
approach – for one thing, he knew many of the owners personally –
altered all this. The P.R.A. acquired a secretary, Lorna Hubbard, to
help him with the immense amount of correspondence involved in the
increasing number of exhibitions at Burlington House – this to the
understandable dismay of Sir Walter Lamb, respected permanent
Secretary of the Royal Academy since 1913, whom some Academicians
felt that Kelly was jostling towards retirement.

'Miss Hubbard' and 'Miss Mansel' became his twin adjutants. Lorna
Hubbard undertook his work for the Academy, but was often at 117
Gloucester Place doing it. Her recollections of the experience parallel
those of Mrs McClintock ('Miss Mansel').

> Working for Sir Gerald was an exhilarating business [writes
> Lorna Hubbard], though not without its tensions. He was in-
> defatigable in the pursuit of his aims, ruthless of idiosyncrasies
> that conflicted with R.A. standards, and merciless towards in-

feriority of any kind. It was exhausting, exasperating – and worth it every time, because he was also unstintingly generous in his recognition of good service given. It was also starred with totally unexpected honours and peripheral pleasures.

Contending, irritatingly frequently, that 'the best is good enough for us, but only just', he sought out the best possible sources of scholarship and advice to serve on committees. The R.A. Council having approved the principle, Sir Gerald collected his advisers (not all of whom were wholly acceptable to the art historians who were his main supporters); endless lists were evolved and advice given on who should approach whom and how; and then the letter-writing began. For every letter written asking for the loan of a picture, at least three were drafted – and it was when it got to the 6th and 7th that one began to 'sit there like a witch exuding a sort of black ink', to quote Sir Gerald, for he was also, in the midst of his passionate pursuit of his aims, surprisingly sensitive.

Once a loan had been agreed, the Secretariat took over all the practical arrangements for transport, insurance, cataloguing, but Sir Gerald had to be kept minutely informed of progress, and should there be any hint of hitch when Bourlet's called, he would rush to the telephone and demand immediate access to the noble owner whose consent he had already received. By that time the advisory committee's work had been done, but members were invited to join the hanging committee for lunch. Although the general pattern was followed, a good hang was always given priority over historical requirements.

Then came the questions of the unfortunate frames and the grubby condition of the pictures that the R.A. skylights revealed so painfully. More letters, suggesting a light clean at a very moderate price. Very soon the picture would go up to Dr Hell, and in due course would return a delicate translation of its former self.

3

The files of the Royal Academy are full of contradictory evidence on the character of its kindly, irascible, generous, pugnacious President.

When Meredith Frampton, R.A., tells him of an eye ailment which prevents him from painting, Kelly recognizes this as the greatest possible disaster and writes immediately to Lord Webb-Johnson, an old friend: 'Here is his reply, which I hope you will regard as encouraging.' Innumerable evidences of acts of kindness occur in Kelly's letters. Yet also in the files are indignant letters from people eminent in the art-world about his 'malignant tongue' and 'offensive remarks'. Close colleagues would often write more in sorrow than in anger, feeling that he was trying to do too much. 'I certainly cannot carry on without the help and friendship of my colleagues,' he says to one of them. And to another, Charles Cundall, R.A., goes a contrite letter in his own hand (undated), arising out of some confrontation on the hanging committee:

> My dear Charles,
>
> My secretary seems to have done away with the letter I dictated & signed some days ago.
>
> I wrote to protest against a suggestion of yours that I was angry & wasn't loving you any more. Nothing could be more falser!
>
> I have liked you for a long long time & you've always done a lot to help me. I'm grateful & this year I've special reasons to love you because you've hung my pictures so beautifully. Just in the very places where they look their very best!
>
> I'm full of thanks – which is very different from what you pretend to believe I'm (or I was) feeling.
>
> > Yours ever,
> >
> > GERALD.

The year 1951 was full of incident. On 15 February the King and Queen and Princess Margaret dined with the President, whose guests included T. S. Eliot and Dame Edith Evans, and afterwards joined a party in the galleries to see the exhibition of *Holbein and other Masters*. The *École de Paris* exhibition was on view at the same time; it had at least been a gesture, though Munnings had not approved, and (in the words of the Academy's annual report) 'M. Picasso's Communistic sympathies caused him to forbid the inclusion of any work of his.' Queen Mary's visit to the summer exhibition on 6 May gave Kelly the opportunity to write a letter to Charles Spencelayh (28 May 1951), whose microscopically detailed genre pictures have pleased so many people. Spencelayh was then 85 but still painting (he died in 1958).

> As a very old admirer of yours I have great pleasure in writing this letter to you.
>
> Last year I had the privilege of taking Queen Mary round the Academy Summer Exhibition and I showed her your pictures, of which she bought two. This year she asked if you were showing

any pictures and I took her to see them. She was delighted with them, but she wanted one in which she herself was represented. You had a charming picture, No. 643, in which there was a crumpled reproduction of her likeness. She did not like this very much, and she asked me to ask you to paint a picture in which her likeness has a prominent place. She asked me to tell you that this is to be regarded as a commission and she said (and it is typical of her kindness) that she thought I should be able to tell you what she wanted in a way that would not offend you. This delicacy is very typical of Queen Mary, and I am sure you will not dream of taking offence.

Will you, then, please execute a picture for Queen Mary such as those two which she bought from you last year, in which shall be a picture of our very dear and lovely Queen Mother?

The file contains two letters from Spencelayh, the first expressing his gratitude and thanks for Kelly's message (31 May), the second saying that Queen Mary was delighted with the picture he painted for her (31 October).

Brian Reade remembers what he calls the 'curious mixture of civility and abruptness' in Kelly, and notes an instance of it at an Academy soirée during his presidency:

I arrived at the top of the staircase, waiting to shake hands with the reception committee [writes Mr Reade], and was thunderstruck by Kelly suddenly saying 'Wait a minute!' So I stood, more or less at ease, while he turned to an attendant behind him holding a towel, in which he proceeded to wipe his hands. Then he turned back to shake my hand and those of the rest of the queue. The same wiping act occurred after the passage of every dozen or so of the guests. I have never seen this done by any other President, before or since.

4

Kelly was preoccupied by the vast proliferation of art students after the war, and the unhealthy relationship, as he saw it, between these students and 'abstract' art. He got his feelings 'off my chest' in a letter to Sir Edward Bridges at the Treasury (13 December 1951):

. . . During the war I lived at Windsor Castle and I got to know very closely Major Phillips, who was in charge of No. 1 Company of the Grenadier Guards, and on one occasion he showed me a briefing he had been given about the special care that should be taken to encourage the young soldier to choose wisely the career he wanted to take up on leaving the Forces. To my amusement one of the professions they were offered was that of 'art', but to be an artist you must have a certain gift – like freckles or red hair – you cannot just become one by diligence.

That an enormous number of young people, on leaving the Forces, elected to 'take up art' is proved by the fact that in 1949, when I asked Sir Walter Lamb to find out the number of art students in this country, he gave me the astonishing figure of 87,000! Of course, I know a good proportion of them were just amusing themselves or killing time, but in so doing they were using up valuable raw materials and costing the taxpayer enormous sums which might have been better invested elsewhere.

Young people are vain and egoistic, and for those who elect to become artists there are no efficiency tests, no technical examinations to be passed. Representational art is out of fashion – partly, perhaps, because any failure or weakness can immediately be seen – but the young painter has only to take refuge in 'abstracts' and no matter what inanities he may commit he is 'home' because there are no standards by which he can be judged. Malcolm Sargent and Sir George Dyson have both pointed out to me that the musical profession does not suffer from this particular trouble: if a student cannot play in tune or keep in time, then he is dropped, but the would-be young painter is on a much safer wicket.

Kelly developed his line of thought on art-teaching, in a manner more conciliatory to modern art, with a lively talk delivered on the B.B.C. Third Programme:

> . . . I think it is bosh to try to teach 'art' and 'taste', to encourage 'sensibility'. But you can teach a student to learn to use his eyes accurately and to analyse what it is he sees. You can develop his skill until he can put down what he sees and not what somebody else has seen and has talked about. And you can teach him the proper control and care of the instruments and materials of his craft, so that he can put on what he thinks is the right colour in what he thinks is the right place so wisely that it will not jump off, nor crack, nor change. . . .
>
> Let me remind you that two very famous people, Pablo Picasso in Barcelona and Henri Matisse of the Beaux-Arts in Paris, were

both brilliantly successful academic prize winners. Their sound training did not prevent them from going whither their daemon led them. And I am happy to learn that Mr Henry Moore and Mr Graham Sutherland have both had a sound training. . . .

In the eighteen-sixties, the intelligent Paris public was shocked by Manet and Monet, and I remember this when I am shocked, or we in the Academy are shocked, by much that we see. Can we be certain that there is not among it all the seeds of the future? The plants must be given light and air, for funny things grow in the dark. . . . (*The Listener*, 24 January 1952.)

Frank McEwen, Fine Arts Officer of the British Council in Paris – who had helped to organize the *École de Paris* exhibition – wrote to congratulate Kelly (18 February 1952) on his 'splendid and generous' broadcast. He added: 'You are a great peace-maker and your fine gestures serving to reunite the antagonistic schools of ancient and modern art, whose divorce seemed so permanently pronounced for the last 50 years, are obtaining quite miraculous results. The fact that these gestures should repeatedly come from the Royal Academy is, I feel forced to say, a great tribute to a noble President.'

5

The sudden death of King George VI in February 1952, was a personal loss to Kelly. A letter of his to the Duke of Portland (11 October 1952), apologizing for having to bother him to lend pictures so often, contained the sentence: 'The Monarch is our Patron, Protector and Supporter, and the late King was pleased to assure me that he was proud of that fact.' The King had, indeed, given exceptional aid to the Royal Academy. The annual dinner of 1952 was cancelled because of his death.

Kelly's relationship as P.R.A. with 'our Honorary Academician Extraordinary', Winston Churchill, had been cordial from the start. On 1 December 1950, he wrote to congratulate him on his 76th birthday: 'I hope you will get that holiday you spoke of. There is no better occupation than painting.' The Academy files next show Kelly complaining to Churchill (11 July 1951) about gossip in the *Daily Express* and *Sunday Express* alleging that Kelly had remarked at an Academy soirée: 'Nowadays only cads are rich.' Kelly denied making the comment and feared its publication could upset the City of London, to which the Academy might have to appeal for financial help. In response,

Churchill said wisely: 'My advice to you would be not to worry about these things too much. There is such a lot of clatter and chatter that one set of it kills the other.'

When Churchill again became Prime Minister, Kelly sent congratulations in the name of the R.A. Council on 30 October 1951, and received the telegraphed reply, 'Thank you so much.' The following modest letter is typed on black-edged mourning notepaper:

10 Downing Street,
Whitehall, S.W.1.
16 March 1952

My dear Kelly,

I have received the notice from the Academy about sending in some pictures for this year. I do not think on any account I could send more than one or two at the outside. Perhaps you would come down one day and pick them out from what I have. My Secretary could arrange with yours. I should of course be very glad to send none at all.

On the other hand I must apprise you of the fact that Lord Alexander has a whole flock of really fine pictures far better than any I have painted, especially in still life, and I am sure it would be a feature in the Academy if you persuaded him to send you a few. I will help you with him if you decide to make an approach.

Yours sincerely,
WINSTON S. CHURCHILL.

Kelly at once followed up Churchill's hint. Three pictures by Earl Alexander of Tunis were hung in the 1952 Academy, and another, a still-life, in the exhibition of 1953. The title of one of the first three, 'From my Studio Window', suggests that Alexander took his painting seriously, as indeed was the case. He had been influenced by the French Impressionists, and by his close friendship with Edward Seago. Alexander's work was distinguished. He might almost have been called a professional painter *manqué*. As an inspired amateur, however, Churchill – at his best – had no need to fear comparison with Alexander as an artist.

6

The exceptional energy of Kelly in his seventies also offered something Churchillian. Always on his own admission a 'chatterbox', his gift of language had crystallized. He proved now that, if he had not succeeded as a painter, he could have triumphed as a journalist, and possibly even as some sort of actor.

In the early nineteen-fifties, I was literary editor of the *Spectator*, and when I invited the overworked P.R.A. to review some books for that paper, I had small hopes of success. I need not have worried. In 1951–2, Kelly found time to contribute several admirable notices to the *Spectator*. He wrote on the forger Van Meegeren, on Lely and Lawrence, on his great favourite Goya, and on a translated selection from the journal of Eugène Delacroix. Always there was that stimulating combination of personal knowledge and driving enthusiasm.

One can understand connoisseurs of a fastidious nature being puzzled by Kelly, perhaps finding it inconvenient to encounter so much knowledge and experience in a P.R.A.; annoying, too, to have to admit that, even at his most infuriatingly dogmatic, he might be right. Probably Kelly tried whenever possible to accept the invitations he received at this time, believing that a successful P.R.A. meant a flourishing Academy. Again, he may have felt that the P.R.A. should 'come eating and drinking'. Accepting the traditional membership of the Athenaeum under Rule 4, he did not use that club nearly as much as Munnings had done; but in 1951 he was fittingly elected a member of The Club, the exclusive dining-club founded by Sir Joshua Reynolds in 1764 to give Dr Johnson an opportunity for conversation. Kelly was eminently 'clubable' in such convivial situations; he enjoyed the dinners for many years and was immensely popular at them. Otherwise his clubmanship was not of the order that demands, like theatregoing, to be termed 'inveterate'. The Bath Club, the Arts, and the Beefsteak all knew him in their season, but he was happiest in his own home and studio.

7

So successful was the Leonardo da Vinci Exhibition, which opened in March 1952, that it had to be extended until September. Much of the profit went to improve the heating system at Burlington House. The organization of a series of lectures on the subject took up some of Kelly's time, and he was pleased when Lord Brabazon consented to take the chair for Dr Ivor Hart's lecture on 'Leonardo and Aeronautics'. He wrote to 'Brab' on 7 April 1952:

> I am so glad you can come: they wanted you so badly, if only for the very human reason that your licence for an aeroplane is No. 1.
> I have presided over most of the lectures: I sit in the centre

armchair in the front row (having come on to the platform with the lecturer) and then listen to my betters. You also will be expected to sit in the front row, and if you would like to make a few preliminary remarks I am sure everyone will be delighted.

A report on a visit of apprentices to the Leonardo Exhibition gave a glimpse of Kelly's style in exposition, soon to become widely familiar:

> At five o'clock Sir Gerald Kelly popped his head round the door of the Reynolds Room in the Royal Academy and said, to no one in particular, 'Where's everybody?' Everybody was present, that is, two hundred apprentices from works throughout the country who had come to see the drawings of the great artificer, Leonardo. 'Come right up,' said Sir Gerald, mounting the dais. 'Come right up and sit on the floor.' And when that was done, and while the attendants were seeing the public out of the galleries, he told the apprentices something of the marvellous native of Vinci, likening the quickness of his eye to that of Denis Compton's. 'Just think,' said Sir Gerald, 'if he had played cricket! Think of the googlies!'
>
> When the galleries were cleared the apprentices swarmed in and gathered in groups round their guides. The lucky ones were those who remained within earshot of Sir Gerald. He has a rare, darting, infectious enthusiasm, and if he kept his group away from drawings of machines they were none the worse for that. 'Just look at these babies!' he said. 'Look at the creases! And look at the lily buds, where the very feel of their crumpled tips is communicated! And look at the child hugging a cat! And look at these doodles, the young head and the old head repeated over and over again, covering sheets.' The apprentices crowded in Sir Gerald's erratic wake, eyes wide open. (*Manchester Guardian*, 8 May 1952.)

After the Leonardo Exhibition, the Diploma Gallery was used for a retrospective exhibition of the art of Sir Frank Brangwyn. The exhibition owed much to the enthusiasm of Kelly himself and of Count William de Belleroche, Brangwyn's long-standing admirer. It was the first one-man show of work by a living artist to be held at the Royal Academy.

Kelly and de Belleroche discussed the exhibition with Brangwyn at Ditchling in July 1952. Brangwyn had always been 'difficult', and at 85 his temper was erratic. He became extremely angry with de Belleroche for drawing Kelly's attention to a picture called 'The Baby Show', which Brangwyn had based on a newspaper illustration and thought little of, but which Kelly, unfortunately, had rather liked.

'Of course you are irritated. I daresay it was my fault,' wrote Kelly soothingly to Brangwyn (26 August 1952), and he continued:

> Walter Sickert used newspaper illustrations a lot I believe and he was a very good artist and his pictures are all Sickerts!
>
> However, I will respect your wishes and 'The Baby Show' will not be seen in our Exhibition. So you can calm down and it is no good getting angry with Willie de Belleroche.

Kelly went on to stress, 'It's going to be a wonderful show,' and added as a postscript, 'I took the trouble to go – personally – to Swansea where I chose *the whole lot* of preliminary drawings they have.* It'll be an eye opener!'

The exhibition was worthy of Brangwyn, but de Belleroche had become disillusioned by his hero's attitude towards him, in this and other instances. After all, he had been Brangwyn's most persistent supporter and collector, had written books about Brangwyn, and even helped to establish a Brangwyn Museum at Bruges. Two years later (9 August 1954) Kelly had to write another soothing letter, this time to de Belleroche's mother. It included some lines born of long experience:

> . . . What you're fussing about I simply don't know.
>
> No one expects old artists like Brangwyn to feel gratitude for more than a few minutes, after which they ease the burden off their shoulders.

* i.e. for Brangwyn's panels in the Guildhall at Swansea originally intended for the House of Lords.

CHAPTER TEN

Television Star

I

Over the years, Kelly painted eighteen portraits of Somerset Maugham. 'The Jester'* of 1911 at the Tate Gallery stands out in its freshness and originality. The next best may be the charming romantic portrait of 1913 belonging to Maugham's daughter Lady Glendevon. No less than fifteen of the remaining portraits have been assembled at the Humanities Research Center of the University of Texas. Kelly painted his first portrait of Maugham in 1907 and the last in 1963, two years before Maugham's death.

In 1949 Graham Sutherland completed a controversial portrait of Maugham which was acquired by the Tate Gallery and soon became famous (or, as some may prefer, notorious). Visiting the Tate in 1952, Cecil Roberts found the Sutherland portrait upstairs and Kelly's 'The Jester' in the basement. When Roberts wrote to Kelly to argue that the arrangement ought to be reversed, Kelly modestly deprecated Roberts' enthusiasm (13 August 1952) and said that his picture 'was done just casually' and was 'just a gay little picture, whereas Graham Sutherland is, they tell me, a very important artist, and his remarkable study of Willie is certainly revealing. To think that I have known Willie since 1902† and have only just recognized that, disguised as an old Chinese Madame, he kept a Brothel in Shanghai!'

As Kelly had studied Maugham's features more closely than anyone else, the flash of sarcasm may be excused; in fact Kelly's relations with Graham Sutherland were most friendly. Maugham had tried, unsuccessfully, to persuade Sutherland to submit his portrait to the Royal Academy. Considering that Kelly was P.R.A., the artist's hesitation was understandable! But Kelly wrote to congratulate Sutherland on

* Plate 7.   † 1903 seems the more likely date. D.H.

receiving the Order of Merit in 1960, and Sutherland wrote to praise a Kelly portrait of Maugham in 1963. In reply to the last letter, Kelly used the enigmatic phrase: 'You and I both know how extraordinarily paintable Maugham is.' It should be added that the caricature element exemplified in Sutherland's portraits of Maugham and Beaverbrook has tended to give way to the representational in his later work.

During the summer of 1952, Kelly was mainly occupied with organizing the exhibition of *Dutch Pictures* (1450–1750) which opened in November. This show lacked the scope of the Academy's Dutch exhibition of 1929; the latter had covered a longer span, and was not confined, like this one, to paintings; in 1952, however, more than 600 wonderful pictures were collected from Great Britain alone, and their choice was entirely the responsibility of the London committee – a colossal task. They were insured for over four million pounds.

While *Dutch Pictures* were his central concern, Kelly was also trying to complete one of his most successful portraits, that of Dr Ralph Vaughan Williams,* commissioned by the Royal College of Music. Sir George Dyson, the Director, hoped the portrait could be received before he retired at the end of the year. Kelly was hindered by lumbago and an internal upset, but he allowed the unfinished picture to go to the College for a presentation ceremony, on condition that he got it back again immediately. Sir George Dyson wrote to him on 17 October 1952:

> My Council saw the portrait yesterday and we all think it simply superb. There is no other word for it, both as a likeness and as a composition. It is just the man V.W. is . . . We are all greatly looking forward to seeing the picture finished and permanently hung in our Council Room.

Vaughan Williams was nearly eighty before it was realized no adequate portrait of the great man existed. Kelly had then been called in to paint him. The sittings were unusual. Kelly described them in an article for the *R.C.M. Magazine*:

> I had seen him many times, slouching, on the platform (for he holds himself anyhow) and of course I had seen many photographs of him but I wasn't prepared to find him so very good looking (he must have been indeed beautiful in his youth), nor was I prepared for his immense bulk. He weighs a packet and is not very steady on his legs – poor things, they have to do a lot of work.

* Plate 9a.

The first difficulty was to get him on to my Model Throne, which is on wheels. So I got a step and tied it to the throne and really made it impossible for it to slip while he made his way, with difficulty, on to the chair. It is a very wide chair; he filled it to bursting and then immediately went to sleep. When he woke up with that sweet smile of his he told me I must not mind if he slept, for he had slept through more good music than any other man that had ever lived.

I made drawings of him. I got Mr Douglas Glass to go down with me to his home in the country and photograph him in all sorts of positions. But he never showed me any of the prints, alleging that they were not good enough. Then I, myself, took a lot of photographs of him but none of them were much good either. I made very careful pencil drawings of his hands as he sat asleep. Mrs Vaughan Williams (whom he had not as yet married) made a suggestion about his hands which I carried out. I used to put him in the chair and literally tie his arms above the wrist to the arms of the chair and let him sleep. I am very proud of the hands and I did them because I had literally hours and hours during which he was comfortable and never moved because he was asleep.

Nobody could say he posed well but curiously enough he did help by providing that sympathy to my enterprise which many sitters lack and which is the principal cause of one's failures. When the picture was finished it was very like what I had wanted to paint. I think it is very like him and I am very proud of it and enjoyed painting it. (*Vol. LI, No. 3, Christmas 1955.*)

Kelly ended his account by recording Mrs Vaughan Williams's 'story' that when V.W. told Kelly he could not come for any more sittings, he (Kelly) had insisted on him leaving his jacket and waistcoat behind, so that he could paint them on a lay figure, and 'according to them, I was quite willing that he should leave my house in his shirt sleeves.' Kelly commented: 'This makes a pleasant tale but I am not quite convinced that it is as they pretend. Anyhow they both tell me that they have pleasant memories of the picture and he claims that I exaggerate the amount he slept.'

The portrait of Vaughan Williams was finished in time to be exhibited at the Academy summer show in 1953. It is not the only portrait by Kelly that hangs in the Royal College of Music, for Kelly presented a portrait of Sir Malcolm Sargent to the College, after the latter's death, in March 1968.

2

In 1952–3 Edward Halliday, the portrait painter, was the 'out-of-vision' newsreel commentator of the B.B.C. Television Service, and its only impresario of the visual arts. Some twelve years earlier, he had organized and 'hosted' a pioneer television visit to the Royal Academy for non-members Varnishing Day at the summer exhibition. Halliday now proposed to Kelly that the B.B.C. should repeat the experiment, and that the President should accompany him round the Dutch exhibition and discourse upon the pictures. Halliday was much liked by Kelly, and when he broached the subject to him Halliday got the impression that the project was acceptable. Accordingly, a transmission time of 9.40–10.10 p.m. on Tuesday, 13 January 1953, was allotted to this important 'live' broadcast. The chosen producer Bill Duncalf set the complex administrative procedures in motion. On 19 December 1952, Duncalf arrived punctually at 10.0 a.m. at Burlington House to meet the President. He was cordially received by Humphrey Brooke, the recently appointed Secretary of the Academy, and Henry Rushbury, the Keeper, both of whom were anxious that the interview should go well. They escorted him to the President's room. What followed is best told by Duncalf:

> The President's secretary, a most charming person, on this occasion greeted us with little enthusiasm [writes Bill Duncalf] and went to the inner sanctum to report my arrival. The message came back that he couldn't see anyone and I would have to come another time. In this wise began my first encounter with this unpredictable little Irishman. As I remember, Henry Rushbury, Kelly's long established and greatly treasured friend, took charge, and eventually I found myself face to face with the President. To my horror, to the embarrassment of Brooke, and to Rushbury's evident amusement, I had my baptism of fire and brimstone. He appeared to be in a cold fury. While apparently busying himself with more important matters littering his table, I was told that the whole idea of television was a disagreeable intrusion, that he was an extremely busy man, and that in any case he had no intention of appearing in front of television cameras.
>
> I became rooted to the floor. The transmission was scheduled for three weeks hence. Already the *Radio Times* billing was due, the full engineering effort was mobilized, and here I was, now

facing disaster and the impossible task of finding a last-minute substitute to fill the gap in our schedule. Of course what I didn't
realize as I quaked there – in my best suit, hair on end, eyes bulg-
ing, with the President and all the furniture swimming about –
was (a) that he was a brilliant actor, and (b) that I was getting a
sample of what I could expect if he didn't have things all his own
way, and unless the B.B.C. clearly understood exactly where it
belonged.

Duncalf was led off by Brooke, who told him not to worry and that
everything would turn out all right – a reassurance he found hard to
accept. However, after consultation with the head of television outside
broadcasts, and with Halliday, it was decided to carry on and pray for a
miracle on the night. Duncalf had been warned that Kelly was consti-
tutionally incapable of being 'produced' or directed, so everything
depended on Edward Halliday; he was the B.B.C.'s trump card; he
would accompany the President on his tour, hold his microphone, and
attempt to keep him in the right place, facing the right way at the right
time.

At a rehearsal on the night before the programme, Duncalf decided
to concentrate entirely on technicalities; he asked Humphrey Brooke
to tell Kelly that he would not be expected to attend, which Brooke
was relieved to be able to do. Yet to Duncalf's horror, when the galleries began to assume an appearance of utter chaos, the President suddenly materialized in the midst of it, scowling beneath his black
broad-brimmed hat.

> I was dumbfounded [writes Bill Duncalf]. This, I felt, would
> now be the end, and I braced myself for battle.
> The President was icy. His biting tone I was getting used to.
> But this was another performance. Precisely, in the most carefully
> chosen phraseology, he informed me that not only had I asked him
> to be there, but that he had even cancelled an important dinner
> date in order to *be* there. I now became exasperated, and in my
> best English and as firmly as my knocking knees would allow, I
> exonerated myself, Humphrey Brooke, and the small army of
> technicians who had temporarily suspended operations to watch
> with gaping mouths, and told him that he had got it wrong and
> shouldn't be in the building. Whereupon he transferred his wrath
> to his private secretary, *in absentia*; looked at me, and then at
> Halliday; instantly softened and said 'Well, never mind, come
> along and have some supper'. In a daze I followed them to the

dining-room where the mighty Hubbocks, major domo and epi-
tome of all the magnificent in butling, awaited us in Windsor
livery beside a sea of dazzling white linen sprinkled with Georgian
silver and cut glass. . . .

3

In the late afternoon of the actual day of the broadcast, 13 January
1953, Kelly and Halliday did have a simple rehearsal or 'walk through',
moving slowly from picture to picture while camera positions and
lighting were finally settled. The galleries were full of men and equip-
ment; the floors a network of cables. It was tiring and irksome. Kelly
had never liked the idea of the programme, and now that he understood what was actually involved, and the conditions under which he
would have to speak, he grew angrier and angrier.

Finally, when Duncalf and Halliday joined him for another delightful
little supper, he exploded. He said he had not realized the pictures
would come out only in black-and-white (!) and so small. He would be
distracted, he felt sure, by the lights, the moving cameras and microphones, and the technicians and floor managers hovering behind them.

'How can you put over great art in this way?' he cried. 'I'm not
going to do it! It's quite ridiculous!'

> You can imagine the effect of this bombshell on Duncalf and
> me! [writes Edward Halliday]. The show was scheduled to go on
> the air in an hour's time . . . What was to be done?
> Duncalf and I did our best to make him change his mind. We
> agreed that the pictures on the screen would be but the poorest
> reproduction of the paintings, but until colour came to television
> it was the best that could be done and still very much worth
> while. If only, we said, he would ignore the lights and cameras
> and microphones and just be himself and talk to me naturally, as if
> he and I were going round the exhibition alone.

'The paintings may not come over so well,' said Halliday, 'but your
personality certainly will!'

'Nonsense!' exclaimed Kelly. 'It is the Dutch paintings the programme is all about, not me!'

In desperation, Halliday played his final card. He recalled that when
he had previously visited the Academy for B.B.C. Television, he had
asked the then President, Sir Edwin Lutyens, to say a few words to a

young artist exhibiting for the first time. Lutyens had agreed, provided Halliday wrote down on a piece of paper what he wanted him to say! But when the young exhibitor – who happened, not surprisingly, to be a very pretty girl in an attractive hat – was brought into the picture, Lutyens found he had forgotten his bit of paper. However, with great gallantry he had improvised, put his arm round the girl's shoulders, looked into her eyes, and said 'Will you be my sweetheart?'

Halliday declared that at that moment the broadcast had suddenly become alive. 'And so, Gerald,' said Halliday beseechingly, 'you do see that, if you are *yourself*, as Lutyens was, and behave naturally, all will be very well?'

The romantic example set by 'Ned' Lutyens may have helped Kelly to respond to the challenge. At all events, he relented. When they went on the air, he was his inimitable self, going from picture to picture making remarks that communicated his enthusiasm and awakened the interest of ordinary people in a way no serious talk on Dutch art could possibly have done.

> Halliday exercised his magic on him to such effect [writes Bill Duncalf] that everyone watching, both at Burlington House and far beyond, was electrified. It is no exaggeration to say that overnight Kelly became a living legend. When I faded the last picture, climbed out of the control van parked in the forecourt and hurried up the grand staircase to congratulate him, I found him surrounded by enthralled riggers and engineers, expatiating on the more intimate anatomical details of a huge Rubens.
>
> After we succeeded at last in tearing him away, we dressed the little man in his black hat, grey scarf, and black overcoat with velvet collar, and walked him down the grand staircase to the entrance. In the vestibule was a group of Press representatives and photographers who had rushed from their television sets. At that moment, Kelly realized what television had done for him, and that henceforth things would never be quite the same. The next day, coming by taxi to Burlington House, he was deeply moved when the cab-driver told him he had watched him the night before and was proud to drive him, and, pointing to the long queue stretching from the doors out into Piccadilly, said 'I reckon you done that.'

4

Those who can speak with authority on a special subject, and at the same time hold the attention of a popular audience, will always be few. Kelly's unpredictability soon became obvious to those who watched his first television appearance. Dozens of press cuttings show that no one

The Evening News, Friday, January 16, 1953   NS 5

LONDON LAUGHS   (No. 5,524)   *By LEE*

" . . . and as I 'eard Sir Gerald say the other day, one can only be lost in wonder at the ruddy blush so skilfully depicted on the maiden's modest cheek."

could guess what he was going to say next – or how he was going to say it. By general agreement, the chief excitement was caused – forty years after *Pygmalion* – by Kelly's spontaneous use of the word 'bloody' (twice). When Halliday, an admirable foil, politely praised a Rembrandt self-portrait, Kelly broke in with: 'My dear fellow, that's a bloody work of genius.' And of Rembrandt's 'Man in Armour', he commented: 'I just go all goo-goo when I stand in front of it. It is one of the finest pictures in the world. In fact, it's a bloody marvel!'

Pointing to a tulip in another picture, he exclaimed: 'Look at that confounded drop of water. Looks as if it might fall off any moment. That's sheer damned skill.' Similarly, a lady painted by Franz Hals was 'a perfect sweetie-pie', and Gerard Terborch's 'Reading the Letter' featured 'another sweetie-pie' (an expression which Lady Kelly tried hard to eradicate from her husband's vocabulary). The programme ran over its scheduled time: 'You know, I get excited and carried away every time I come here,' said Kelly.

The *Daily Express* reporter was in Burlington House before the programme went off the air. The *Daily Mail* man came hot on his heels, and asked Kelly about that controversial adjective. 'Nonsense!' replied the President. 'I quoted Rembrandt. It was Dutch.' Back at 117 Gloucester Place, the house was under siege; the telephone never stopped ringing. Jane asked a reporter from the *Daily Herald* to answer the calls from the other newspapers.

Next morning the man at Halliday's garage was putting petrol into his car when he said: 'I seen you on the telly last night.' 'Did you? What did you think of it?' asked Halliday. The garage man replied: 'That chap with you loved them photos, didn't he?'

The evening made Kelly a television star, and certainly he had no regrets for it, especially when he saw the crowds pouring into *Dutch Pictures*. His uninhibited language had probably assisted his purpose of arousing attention. As Thomas Barnes, the great editor of *The Times*, said in the eighteen-thirties, 'John Bull whose understanding is rather sluggish . . . requires a strong stimulus . . . you must fire ten-pounders at his densely-compacted intellect before you can make it apprehend your meaning or care one farthing for your efforts.'

But it is notable that, whereas many people had telephoned to object to Munnings' sensational speech of 1949, no one complained to the B.B.C. about Kelly's programme on *Dutch Pictures*. On the contrary, most of the viewers were so fired by his enthusiasm that they forgave him his adjectives; many wrote to ask for more of Gerald Kelly. The

Express and the *Mail*, like Tweedledum and Tweedledee, fought a
formal battle over his language: the *Express* deprecated, but the *Mail*
excused. C. A. Lejeune had the last and best word:

> Who in the world could have guessed in advance that the most
> sensational programme of the fortnight would be a conducted tour
> round the Dutch pictures at the Royal Academy? Yet it was so
> . . . By the mercy of Providence, I kept my set on, and by jingo!
> it was worth it. The president, Sir Gerald Kelly, has already be-
> come almost as celebrated as Mr Gilbert Harding for the naughty
> things he said. I liked them fine; but even better I liked the *good*
> things he said; the way he gave one the *feeling* of a picture, the
> texture, the atmosphere, the length, breadth and thickness, and
> the excitement or affection behind each individual painting . . .
> I'd call this, by and large, one of the most exciting transmissions
> of the past year. (*The Observer*, 18 January 1953.)

5

The public has been so thoroughly exposed to television since 1953
that no individual performance could now create such a sensation as
Kelly's did. But for the friends who had long known in private the 'blue
streak' of Kelly's talk (to use Dr Hilles' expression), it was no surprise
to find him hailed by millions as a 'natural'.

Those who encountered Kelly personally may be placed in three
categories: first, those lucky enough to get on well with him from the
start; second, those who had an abrasive experience to begin with and
never advanced beyond it; third, those who may have been initially
stung by caustic criticism or a peevish outburst, but who persevered,
learned to value Kelly's integrity, and eventually became good friends
of his.

Before the events of January 1953, Edward Halliday had already
passed through the flame. 'If Gerald found something to like, he said so
with great generosity and in words no less uncertain than those he used
to condemn,' writes Halliday. 'Many young painters, myself included,
gained much from both aspects of his criticism and owed much to his
encouragement. I grew to love the little man. I stood up to him and we
argued a great deal.'

For Bill Duncalf, the organizer of the nerve-wrecking preparations
and eventual triumph of Kelly's first television programme, the lesson

was the same. For several years after that momentous evening Duncalf, as he says, 'held the appointment of B.B.C. Producer Extraordinary to the Kelly Household. At times it was a mixed blessing, but one on which I can now look back in fond appreciation.' He treasures a small Kelly oil painting of a Burmese street scene. It is inscribed by the artist on the back 'For Bill, with affection.'

For Kelly himself, propelled into the limelight overnight at the age of 73, the evening of 13 January also had its lessons. The medium he despised had been shown capable of serving the appreciation of art, and of bringing crowds to Burlington House. He wrote frankly about his conversion:

> As for television, I remember how shocked I was when first asked to do a programme, and how doubtful I was whether such a thing should be attempted, would be wise, or even feasible. How ignorant I was! Now I know that, owing to the marvellous images which can be shown on the television screen, it is the ideal way of bringing pictures into the homes of hundreds and hundreds of people, thus giving them a new source of pleasure and entertainment to which they might otherwise have no access. Pictures are one of my passions: looking at them is for me a relaxation and a delight, a delight which I want to share with as many people as possible. If television can bring it to people living out of reach of London, or to those who are for some reason unable to get about very easily, then I am glad to be the man to talk to them because although it may perhaps ill become me to say so, I do wax enthusiastic about paintings, and sincere enthusiasm can be communicated. (*Radio Times*, 11 December 1953.)

As Kelly continued to appear on television, he was recognized by more and more people in the street – especially by the drivers of the many taxis he used. Kelly's article went on:

> How touched I was, how very touched, when one day, when I was paying him, a taxi-driver said, 'I know who you are. I saw you on television, and I went to see the pictures and I liked them – some of them, anyway.' I was so glad he did not say he had liked them all, for I shouldn't have believed him, and when he admitted that there were some he didn't care for, it meant that he had really liked the others.

Dr Ralph Vaughan Williams, 1952 (oil, 35″ × 45″).

T. S. Eliot, 1962
(oil, 47″ × 36″).

W. Somerset Maugham sitting to Kelly in his studio.

Bust of Gerald Kelly
by Maurice Lambert,
R.A.

CHAPTER ELEVEN

Struck by Lightning

I

During the closing stages of the Dutch Exhibition, the President and Lady Kelly gave a dinner at Burlington House for Queen Elizabeth II and the Duke of Edinburgh (10 February 1953), at which the Queen sat between Kelly and Somerset Maugham. Mr and Mrs Winston Churchill were also there.

On 26 February, Kelly received Queen Juliana of the Netherlands, when she visited *Dutch Pictures*, having himself previously been invested at the Netherlands Embassy with the insignia of Commander in the Order of Orange Nassau. Kelly had long before (1950) been made a Commander of the French Legion of Honour, joining Maugham in a distinction which the latter assured him he would find of great service whenever he was travelling in France.

At the annual Academy dinner on 30 April – a rainy day, with austere cold beef on the menu again – Kelly took the chair and Winston Churchill (who spoke first), Lord Alexander, Sir Harold Nicolson, and Sir Alan Herbert were the principal guests. Churchill's intervention with Kelly on behalf of Lord Alexander had given the latter considerable pleasure, as his speech showed:

> . . . When I was a boy I had three ambitions [said Lord Alexander]. One was to win the V.C. which I didn't; the other was to be a rugger international which I wasn't; and the third was to be an R.A. or to be precise, P.R.A. But I'm afraid that I have left that rather too late. Nevertheless, I have salvaged something out of the wreck of my early ambitions because, at least, I have had more than one of my paintings accepted and hung in the summer Exhibition at Burlington House.

Kelly had always admired Harold Nicolson as writer and speaker. Nicolson's diary account of this dinner shows him excessively modest:

> I am placed at the top table [wrote Harold Nicolson] between the French and Portuguese Ambassadors. I eat no dinner and sip no drink . . . I repeat my piece all right, but it is *not* liked . . . the impression I give is one of nervous pomposity . . . I return miserable and humiliated to Albany.

Sir Alan Herbert spoke next. Addressing himself to Kelly, he said:

> As for you, sir, I've been drubbing about in the art world, and I can tell you this, that all men speak well of you. One man speaks of the numerous fine paintings you have made of the beautiful Jane. The next man says – 'Oh yes, the *Daily Mirror* man.'* Another says – 'Yes, I can always tell a Kelly' – perhaps the greatest tribute of all . . . Others tell me that at Cambridge University, you won, with great pride and properly, the Winchester Reading Prize, which is generally won by such men as Pitt, and Palmerston, Francis Bacon, and Isaac Newton. Others speak of the fine and patient work of restoration which you've done at Dulwich. All agree that as President of this fine affair, you have led, and inspired and planned like a Churchill, you've led like an Alexander, and that you have been as kind and as catholic as a Nicolson in everything that you have done . . . let us lift our glasses and drink to the Royal Academy of Arts, and link with that toast, the name of its illustrious President, Sir Gerald Kelly.

The President's speech at this dinner was typical of him. It aired his thoughts on modern art; his love of enthusiasm – and of cricket; pride in the independence of the Royal Academy and its Schools; distrust of State aid in art-teaching. Kelly declared he had planned 'a great discourse' in justification of the Royal Academy, but that morning had read in *The Times* an article conceding all he was proposing to claim. He went on:

> . . . I do not mind the doubts about what artists and critics feel concerning the precise connection between the Royal Academy and Art.
>
> One of the functions of this Royal Academy is to provide an impenetrable citadel for those morally brave people who dare to

* The *Daily Mirror* was then publishing a strip cartoon featuring the adventures of a girl called Jane.

confront fashion. Do you know, throughout the year I receive a remarkably large mail, some friendly, some otherwise, but the letters that bother me are those that ask for help and advice on how to understand Modern Art.

The worst of it is, I can do nothing to help them. For what I think these people really want is a prescription against being thought wrong.

Against making mistakes. I think they are frightened lest their own opinions should not earn them social credit. From my superb, but still-born, and never-to-be-published discourse I will resurrect one phrase: 'Mistakes do not matter.'

It makes no difference how often one is wrong. It does not matter what one admires. The stimulus is not the important thing. The *important* thing is the emotion. As Shakespeare very nearly said, 'A little of what you fancy does you good.' Personally, if you will allow me to speak in my own person, I am a little bothered at the vast ouput of works now being produced in Patagonia, in Iceland, in Tierra del Fuego, and in London, which seem to me to demand no beauty of expression or technical skill.

I am a naughty old man, utterly unrepentant in my love of things beautifully done. When I stand in front of . . . a Rembrandt or a Velasquez, I am as thrilled as if I was watching Len Hutton driving through the covers. Or Denis Compton, driving to leg. One sees the thing done. It is breathtakingly beautiful. But one doesn't know how it was done.

And I know that those of you who, like myself, like watching cricket, know that Compton and Hutton could never have produced those beautiful strokes if they had only been instructed by an intellectual sitting in the pavilion, who himself had never picked up a bat. They acquired the skill that thrills us, after hours of exacting practice in the nets, and it is at the nets that the cricketers of the world have been taught, and it is in the academic schools that the artists of the future should be trained. I do hope for the last minute or two I have not been at silly point.

Personally, for what that may be worth, I think the visual arts are in a little bit of a mess. I think they are muddled, intellectually, but I hope that after the revolution, and revolutions have never done any more than shift a burden, from some one thing to another thing, there will come perhaps to be born in England our saviour, another genius, another Rubens, another Raphael, or lest you don't quite follow what I'm saying, another Turner. But he will have to be, in addition to his artistic genius, a very tough and obstinate nut. Tough so as to withstand the pressure brought to bear on him; I will not say from whom – but the whole of modern culture insists upon bringing pressure to bear on the young, and oh, how wicked it is; when that saviour comes – perhaps I, seated on a little cloud, dressed like one of Murillo's later angels, shall look down and see this promising genius taking refuge in an academic school, from the cloud of help that is being offered to him so strenuously from State Aid.

2

The Spring of 1953 was the time set for the re-opening of the Dulwich Gallery, to which Kelly had given anxious care for nearly ten years. It had been a daunting task to superintend the cleaning, reassembling, re-framing and hanging of the pictures in the rebuilt Soane gallery, and their cataloguing, identifying and transport. 'The movements of the pictures gave us every opportunity for confusion and dismay,' says Kelly's secretary Miss Mansel; 'I was always trying to straighten out our lists of their whereabouts.' The official re-opening not only came as a relief, but was a very proud moment in Kelly's life; nor did his interest in the gallery diminish thereafter.

Exalted company, great occasions and merited honours may be considered traditional privileges of Presidents of the Royal Academy. But no earlier president had made himself a television star overnight. As the hour approached for Kelly's next appearance 'on the box', there was newspaper speculation. The occasion was a tour on 15 May of the Academy exhibition of *Kings and Queens* assembled in honour of the Coronation. Kelly had Sir Owen Morshead as his companion, and they enjoyed this joint effort (Plate 11a).

Naturally Kelly was aware of the repercussions of the uninhibited language he had used in January. He knew that millions of viewers were watching him with bated breath. He solved his major problem rather neatly. As Peter Black said:

> The question was: Would he use the colloquialism that fell from his lips at the Dutch exhibition? The answer was a compromise. Sir Gerald, looking as much as ever like an extremely knowing secretary bird, remarked of Holbein's portrait of Mary Tudor: 'I always call her "Bloody Mary". I think it's in my role to say that.'

Sir Owen Morshead, chief librarian of Windsor Castle, smiled and said: 'And it's in my role to appear shocked.' (*Daily Mail*, 16 May 1953.)

The papers reported the programme in detail. It seems to have been the last time Kelly employed that dangerous adjective on television. His individual flow of language continued freely, but its use became slightly more controlled. Queen Henrietta Maria received the comment: 'I am not allowed to say sweetie-pie. So I shall call her a poppet.' Of Philip of Spain he said, 'Nasty-looking face, isn't it?' and of the amorous Charles II: 'What manhood! How busy he was! They were so glad to have him back after all those confounded Puritans.'

The programme ended on a mysterious note. A painting by Kelly of the Imperial Crown was shown. 'Painters don't get much chance to get near it,' said Kelly, 'but I had the luck at Windsor to do so.' Morshead added: 'I remember with what trepidation I handed it over to you.' Kelly continued: 'I spent day after day painting it. Do you remember the time I very nearly lost it?'

After this, Kelly dried up abruptly, as if he felt he might have said too much.

> Five million viewers were left flat in the middle of the story of how Sir Gerald nearly lost the Crown of England. The secret remained with him last night. A voice on the telephone at his West-End home said: 'Sir Gerald got back very tired and we sent him straight to bed.'* (*News Chronicle*, 16 May 1953.)

3

Besides his admirable portrait of Vaughan Williams, Kelly had portraits of the Lord Chancellor (Lord Simonds), Sir Hubert Houldsworth, and Dr Marie Stopes in the 1953 Academy. In July he visited Belgium to discuss the loan of pictures for the great exhibition of *Flemish Art 1300–1700* which he was planning for the following winter.

When a balustrade in the courtyard of Burlington House was slightly damaged by lightning, Somerset Maugham wrote to Kelly (28 July 1953):

> Knowing how irascible you are I knew at once that it was you who had struck Burlington House with lightning. If you will allow

* Subsequent inquiries hardly suggest that the Crown was at serious risk.

me to say so, you showed a certain amount of inexperience with your thunderbolt since you don't seem to have damaged any of the Academicians, but only a bit of stonework. Better luck next time.

Maugham's comment was friendly cynicism, based on thorough knowledge. Those working at Burlington House with this enthusiastic trenchant character were in constant danger of being struck by the presidential lightning. Perhaps the expert advisers who served on the committees assembled for winter exhibitions like the Flemish were in most danger. Kelly would wholly disregard professional advice (often no doubt rightly) if he did not care for it, and when the charm was not in evidence, he could be disconcertingly offensive. It may be that these bands of art-historians proved difficult and temperamental; they may have driven Kelly distracted; but there were some among them who felt they deserved better – and who, in a phrase Kelly would have appreciated, 'retired hurt', preferring to avoid a second innings.

If Kelly would usually hang the pictures as he thought best, without too much regard to scholarly opinion, this may have been because he regarded each undertaking primarily from an artist's standpoint. In his preface to the catalogue of the Flemish Exhibition, Kelly thanked his many helpers, but added the impish sentence: 'P.S. Some credit is due to the painters who produced these lovely things!'

Kelly was accused of stealing the limelight in these splendid exhibitions. The charge is hardly relevant, for without his egotism, enterprise and powers of persuasion the shows would never have come into existence, to give pleasure to millions. Sidney Hutchison's comparison of Kelly to one of the old actor-managers is more interesting; it would have been no use telling Martin-Harvey to get out of the limelight in *The Only Way;* and once Kelly was launched on his television course, there was no one else in the world who could have brought great art to the people in the way he did.

Yet again, before the televising of the Flemish exhibition, the newspapers speculated whether 'verbal fireworks' could be expected. The *Evening Standard* telephoned 117 Gloucester Place in the course of the day (15 December) and was told by 'a private secretary' that Kelly was painting, but that perhaps later, 'when the light went', he could be persuaded to talk on the telephone.

Sir Gerald did talk – in an abrupt impatient manner [said the *Standard*]. Could we expect a repetition of January's lively performance this evening?

Said Sir Gerald severely: 'I certainly hope not. It would have

been intolerable last time if it had not been completely spontaneous.' . . .

Is he looking forward to the broadcast? He replied bluntly: 'I
hate it. It terrifies me.'

This broadcast was one of Kelly's most successful. The B.B.C.
provided him with a glamorous studio manager, Sheila Blower, as an
assistant, and he also had Henry Rushbury to accompany him round the
galleries. The critics were more delighted than ever:

> So long as Sir Gerald is available no one will ever lay complaints
> about too many visits to the Royal Academy (*News Chronicle*).
> It was a fine television performance. He is an enthusiast who can
> communicate his enthusiasm in uncommonly good English (*Daily
> Mail*).
> Sir Gerald Kelly was splendid value last night (*Evening News*).
> It is hardly to be doubted that the P.R.A. made a great hit with
> viewers (*The Listener*).
> By far the most electrifying TV performance of the week (*News of
> the World*).

Jonah Barrington in the *Daily Sketch* relished Kelly's unprofessional
'asides' to the cameramen: 'Are you ready?' 'Hurry up!' 'I suppose I
must trip over this thing.' Above all, he remembered his walk: 'While
his footsteps were pounding the floor there was no doubt who was
boss.'

The broadcast made it clear that, contrary to first impressions,
Kelly's success on television had been a triumph of good language rather
than bad. (The secret of his magnetism, Humphrey Brooke believed,
was 'his Irish command of simple language applied to great works of
art'.) The worst he achieved this time was to mention that a masterpiece from Bruges had once been used as a chopping-block for eels, and
then to turn away briskly with the comment: 'Oh well, to hell with
eels.'

'Sir Gerald Kelly shows himself to be a first-class art salesman every
time he appears on TV,' said the *Star* (18 December). 'His first appearance early this year sent unprecedented numbers hurrying to the Royal
Academy's Dutch exhibition and since he guided viewers round the
Flemish pictures on Tuesday people have kept the turnstiles busy.
Friday is not normally a good day, but today, with only a week to
Christmas and fog lurking around, attendances were far larger than
usual. So many people made straight for the paintings that Sir Gerald
described that it was often difficult to get a look at some of them.'

CHAPTER TWELVE

Churchill and Kelly

I

In 1952 Sir John Rothenstein wrote of Augustus John that 'before he was twenty he had become the first draughtsman in England', and that 'in his inspired moments no living British painter so nearly approaches the grandeur and radiance of vision, the understanding of the human drama, or the power of hand and eye of the great masters of the past.' Kelly and Augustus John were near-contemporaries (John was a year older), and in the nineteen-twenties John was elected first A.R.A., then R.A., shortly before Kelly in each case. Kelly's admiration for John as an artist was of long standing; they were not intimate friends, but they had common enthusiasms, for Rembrandt and Goya, among others (John's obsession with El Greco was less fortunate); and we have seen that in 1926 Kelly was able to give his awkward friend Hugh Walpole an introduction to John. Surviving letters in Lady Kelly's collection show them corresponding in 1930–31 about a French painter's medium in which they were both interested. They also discuss the operations of the Chantrey Bequest, with which Kelly was already concerned. In one letter John writes: 'The Yeats portrait is my property'; and in another 'When I have a thing perhaps worthy of the Tate I would like to show it to you.' Several works by John are now in the Tate Gallery, and one of them is a portrait of W. B. Yeats bought by the Chantrey Bequest in 1940.

John resigned from the Academy in 1938 because a portrait of T. S. Eliot by Wyndham Lewis was rejected, but he allowed himself to be reinstated in 1940. Kelly voted for him at the presidential election of 1944, when Munnings was elected, and always showed himself anxious to conciliate John and the Academy. It comes as no surprise therefore that Augustus John should have been chosen as the second living artist, after Brangwyn, to be honoured by a retrospective exhibition in the Diploma Gallery. Kelly took the lead in organizing the exhibition in the early months of 1954, and John wrote to him on 15 February:

> I enjoyed my visit very much & was on the whole *very* pleased with the works you have collected. In some cases agreeably surprised by the appearance of some of the exhibits which looked much better than I expected. My only criticism is that the walls seemed somewhat crowded. This I think could be corrected by a more severe weeding out of the early drawings, many of which could be dispensed with to advantage & would allow more space for the pictures . . . I noticed with appreciation that most of my suggestions made to Tommy Earp have been acted upon . . .* Once again, thank you for all you have done.

Kelly may have thought more highly of 'the early drawings' than John did. In this connection Lorna Hubbard notes an example of that acute sensitivity which co-existed with apparent ruthlessness in Kelly's character. He so much appreciated the drawings as a complete reflection of the early years that he insisted that Dorelia John and the family should be allowed to enjoy the exhibition in complete privacy. The lift had to be worked for them, but they had the Diploma Gallery to themselves.

The Pied Piper element in Kelly was now often evident. The Academy files contain a letter from a boy (27 April 1954): 'Dear Sir Gerald,' Thank you very much for the exhibition of Augustus John's paintings and drawings, which I have visited today. It was purely because of your remarks in the television newsreel in March, urging young people especially to come to the exhibition . . .'

The strain of his continual exertions was beginning to tell as Kelly approached his seventy-fifth birthday, the statutory limit for every P.R.A. Sir Alfred Munnings, a few months his senior, wanted him to know that he was forgiven for relaxing the Academy's implacable attitude towards modern art and sponsoring the *École de Paris* exhibition: 'I can't forget that you said last night on the phone, that you are getting so that you forget &c &c. Well – I'm sure you remember a lot & *we all* owe you a lot.' (2 March 1954.)

---

* Thomas Earp, author and journalist, wrote an appreciation of Augustus John published as early as 1934. With Kelly, Henry Rushbury, and Hugo Pitman, he served on the executive committee for the exhibition.

2

On 19 February, Kelly wrote to Sir Winston Churchill to invite him to speak at the annual dinner: 'It would break my heart if you could not speak at my last Academy Dinner.' The files of the Royal Academy show that several letters passed between 10 Downing Street and Burlington House during the next few weeks, Churchill's letters affording evidence of his pleasure and modesty in the role of 'Honorary Academician Extraordinary'.

> 10 Downing Street,
> Whitehall.
> 5 March 1954

My dear Sir Gerald,

Thank you for your letter, and for inviting me to the Academy Dinner on April 28. Subject to some unforeseen exigency arising, I should very much like to come, and I will certainly respond for Her Majesty's Ministers.

I wonder if you could lunch with me at Chartwell, on Saturday, March 13? I shall be alone, and we could talk about pictures for the Summer Exhibition.

> Yours very sincerely,
> WINSTON S. CHURCHILL.

On 15 March, Kelly wrote to ask the Prime Minister's advice on the choice of speakers for the dinner, and received the following reply:

> March 28 1954

My dear Sir Gerald,

I have been very hard pressed since you wrote to me, and I am afraid I can contribute very few ideas. I should think Lord Goddard, the Lord Chief Justice, would make a very good speech, and he is a remarkable figure. For the Air I should try to get Lord Portal of Hungerford. He may be willing to come. He is of course the outstanding figure in the Air. I think you are better qualified than I to decide about 'the other arts'!

I shall be sending you some pictures tomorrow afternoon. It was so kind of you to come down and help me pick them out. *Four* is all I mean to have, provided indeed you can find four which you and your colleagues think are good enough.

> Yours very sincerely,
> WINSTON S. CHURCHILL.

When Kelly proposed changes in the pictures chosen, after the Hanging Committee had seen them at the Academy, Churchill agreed at once. He decided that three pictures would now be enough for him to show.

6th April 1954

My dear Sir Gerald,

Thank you for your letter of April 2. I think you are quite right about both the pictures you mentioned, and I am content that only the other three should be shown. If, however, you think the one of the Venetian Islands is better than the Valley in the Atlas, I will send it to you, but I do not wish to have more than three pictures hung. Thank you so much for the trouble you have taken.

Yours very sincerely,

WINSTON S. CHURCHILL.

One surmises that Kelly was not going to let him off so lightly. In the end Churchill did have four pictures in the exhibition, and they included both 'A Valley in the Atlas 1950' (a sketch) and one called 'Near Venice'.

It was entirely owing to Munnings that Churchill was brought happily into the Academy's affairs. Churchill appreciated his painting and his gusto. Nevertheless, in character Churchill perhaps had more in common with Kelly. Like Churchill, Kelly could be ruthless, but in charge of a great institution he showed gifts of administration, initiative, and perseverance, which Munnings had lacked; and what he said in public or wrote for publication proved to be less diffuse, more intelligent. Again, Churchill and Kelly had artistic ideas in common; both were admirers of Monet and Sargent; both were friends of Sickert; neither disdained the aid of photography.

The other speakers at the dinner on 28 April – again a meal of cold beef, for Kelly persisted in official austerity – were highly distinguished but did not include those proposed by Churchill. They were Air Chief Marshal Sir William Dickson, Dr E. D. Adrian (later Lord Adrian), and Sir Arthur Bliss – who composed a fanfare 'Salute to Painting' which was dedicated to Kelly and played at the dinner.

In his speech Churchill paid Kelly a warm tribute:

It is with genuine regret that we face the fact tonight that this is the last Royal Academy Dinner over which Sir Gerald Kelly will preside. The Presidents of the Royal Academy are esteemed figures in British life; none has been more tireless in his search for the welfare of the Academy and of British art in general than Sir

Gerald. During his Presidency we have had the Dutch exhibition and the Flemish exhibition; seldom, if ever, have there been exhibitions at Burlington House which surpassed or even equalled them, either in the quality of the pictures or of the crowds they attracted. For these remarkable selections of paintings we have Sir Gerald's personal labours and persistence to thank. His successor will take over the Presidency at a very high level of its popularity and acclaim . . .

Kelly said the Royal Academy were 'proud to have given so great an exhibition of Flemish art', and he added:

I personally am as pleased as Punch at the success which is attending the exhibition of Augustus John's drawings and paintings. The old lion, alas, is not with us tonight, but his work is there upstairs . . . He is, I am certain, the outstanding figure in the painting, above all in the drawing, of my time.

Before he sat down, Kelly pleaded with his influential audience that the National Gallery and the British Museum should be restored to their regular working order which they had not known since before the war. He reminded them that the P.R.A. was a Trustee of the British Museum ('I know it sounds funny, but he is'), and declared it was scandalous that these institutions 'should be starved into semi-impotence, be prevented by want of money from performing those very duties for which they were designed . . . Sir Winston, Mr Attlee – I can't say Mr Butler because he isn't here, but Mr Gaitskell, can't you do something? . . . Perhaps I have spoken out of turn; I promise never to do so again here.'

Although he was to remain President until the election in December, Kelly now received letters expressing regret at his impending departure. One of these came from Lord Hore-Belisha (17 May 1954):

I had not realized that this was your last year [he wrote]. I am so sorry to read it. But you have behind you an exceptionally active & inspiring record & I congratulate you on all you have done to bring an artistic consciousness home to the public & I wish you well.

Hore-Belisha had qualities discernible in Kelly: courage, drive, impatience. Liddell Hart wrote that those who worked closely with Hore-Belisha often felt exasperation, 'but there were those who found that with deepening association it gave way to a growing blend of admiration and affection'. The same was true of Kelly.

3

Under the will of Sir Francis Chantrey, the Royal Academy received a magnificent bequest, which became available in 1875, for the regular purchase of British paintings and sculpture. In 1897 the works so far acquired by the Academy Council were transferred to the newly opened Tate Gallery. Thenceforward the operation of the bequest became a continual source of friction between the Academy and the Tate; a fact hardly surprising, as these institutions came increasingly to represent the right and left wings of the art world.

The nostalgic display of the whole Chantrey collection at Burlington House in 1949 eased the quarrel. As an historical report on late Victorian and Edwardian taste, the Chantrey exhibition was unique. For Sir Alfred Munnings it provided a sentimental orgy. But it finally established that many (though by no means all) of these former 'pictures of the year' were no longer worth keeping on permanent exhibition. Some people thought the 'modern' acquisitions sponsored by the Tate were still less uplifting. Nevertheless, it was rightly agreed that in future the Tate and the Academy should be equally represented on the recommending committees, and that works should not be purchased without an assurance that the Tate Trustees would accept them.

In 1954, the Tate was in a turmoil. A malicious campaign had been launched against its Director, Sir John Rothenstein – who wrote in his autobiography *Brave Day Hideous Night*:

> We received much sympathy in those days. Perhaps the mark of sympathy that I most of all appreciated came from a man with whom I had been warring over the Chantrey Bequest, the President of the Royal Academy. In view of our past relations it was natural that some Academicians should have considered taking advantage of the Tate's disarray. Sir Gerald Kelly told me that there was indeed one member of his establishment who was working the thing up, but he was not going to have anything of it, he said, and he would publicly denounce any such move. I was deeply affected by this. Sir Gerald and I had clashed very fiercely at Chantrey meetings, and I knew him to be a rudely combative man, but he was a man, the contrary of most of us, capable of being irascible over small issues but splendidly magnanimous over large ones.

Rothenstein was introduced to Kelly by Kenneth Clark within an hour of taking up his duties as Director of the Tate in June 1938. He and Kelly were fated to confront one another, but they had in common a wide knowledge and deep love of painting. The controversy over Graham Sutherland's portrait of Winston Churchill (presented to Churchill on his eightieth birthday in November 1954) brought them together in a cartoon by David Low. Here Rothenstein referees a fight between Sutherland and Lord Hailsham, while Kelly broadcasts a commentary for 'Royal Academy TV' ('Oh, bloody good chiaroscuro, sir!'). Low had captured Kelly even more effectively in *The Art Market*, a cartoon of 1953.

4

On 13 August 1954, Kelly wrote to Kenneth Clark:

> . . . I'm just off to my usual cure in black mud at Abano and hope to come back to a successful final autumn . . . I've had a very tempestuous summer: visits to Paris which were ticklish affairs; one serious operation which meant three weeks in hospital and a nasty septic sore throat, so I personally am feeling about a *hundred* and seventy-five, and only too glad to be relieved of a burden that threatens to overwhelm me.

A few weeks earlier (6 July), he had written to Anne Coleman (now Mrs Knowles), organizer of the Bedford College Art Society, who had invited him to speak to them:

> They have just operated on me and although I have stood the operation extremely well I have not regained much vitality and I am very much inclined to say 'No'.
>
> If you could wait until our next Winter Exhibition has been hung (mid-November) then I think you might find I would quite like to do it. I have got a way with me and I might be very funny but I should loathe to give a demonstration of an extinct volcano.

There was no danger of Kelly imitating an extinct volcano – though he never did manage to get to Bedford College – and throughout the summer he was extremely busy preparing the next winter exhibition, *European Masters of the Eighteenth Century*.

Lorna Hubbard, his secretary at Burlington House, has preserved a vivid dossier of her correspondence with the President at this time: a remarkable example of expert concentration by Kelly on a special aim, and of loyal and intelligent co-operation from Miss Hubbard. Several of Kelly's letters were written during stays in Paris while he was tracking down works by artists such as Fragonard, Chardin, Watteau, and Boucher. He visits a long succession of owners, dealers, museum directors; he mentions 'a staggering sheet of women's heads' by Watteau and a 'great Ingres which I've longed to see all my life'. There are exciting successes and bitter disappointments.

'I'm very, very tired,' he tells Miss Hubbard in one letter. 'The rather dog-eared sheet which I enclose will give you a rough idea of how much or how little I've done. My taxi account would raise your hair & curl it.' A long annotated list of lenders and pictures was enclosed.

'Keep your fingers crossed. There are still some tough guys to deal with,' says another note. And of a certain dealer he writes: 'He is an old man who wants to go slow. I'm an old man who wants to go fast.' One wonders who else in England would have had the enthusiasm, drive and sheer knowledge to tackle the French art world in the way Kelly did – not only at 75, but at any age?

5

The exhibition of *European Masters of the Eighteenth Century* proved a great success, and Kelly's television tour of the galleries on 26 November brought him a letter which he specially valued and carefully preserved:

> Banks Way Farm,
> Effingham Common, Surrey.
> 27–11–54

Dear Sir Gerald,

Forgive me for intruding on your time, but I cannot resist thanking you, for your programme on Television last night.

It was *sheer delight*, and if I may say so, I too can cry, in seeing such beauty as those paintings radiate.

It was a feast for the eyes, the mind; and I am deeply grateful to you.

Thank goodness! amid the turpitudes, and 'inanités' of the usual moron programmes on TV, sometimes one gets a glimpse of beauty, and pleasure.

Thank you, and forgive me for writing. It is not in my habit to write about programmes, but this is stronger than my will. I must thank you.

In great admiration,

YVONNE ARNAUD.

At the election for a new President of the Academy on 7 December, the architect Professor A. E. Richardson was elected by a large majority. Kelly then received the following letter:

> Fryern Court,
> Fordingbridge, Hants.
> Dec. 12 1954

My dear Kelly,

Allow me to congratulate you on your retirement from a position which you have filled with such notable distinction during your Presidentship. Without speaking of my own Exhibition which you alone made memorable, you have let in a great current of fresh air into the precincts of the R.A. and thus dissipated a certain atmosphere of mystery and almost religious seclusion, which had, in later years, accumulated round the person of its President. In a word you have succeeded in humanizing an Institution which, like the artists who compose it, should never allow itself to retire into the false security of the privileged, the unapproachable and the jejune.

I was reading lately the *Journal* of a French author whom I greatly admire, Paul Léautaud, who speaks very appreciatively of an English artist he came to know and sit for in Paris. This artist was named *Kelly* and I wonder if he is alluding to you, which according to the dates and his estimate of you, might well be the case. I don't know your successor, but from what I gather, he is a most charming & sympathetic character & will do the R.A. credit. I am off this week to the south of Spain to complete my convalescence after a very successful Op.

> Yours very sincerely,
> AUGUSTUS JOHN.

The retiring President's farewell was postponed until the end of January 1955, when he had another television appointment, this time to describe some of his favourite pictures in Gallery X of the eighteenth-century exhibition. Once again the critics noted that this 'spry, puckish unpredictable must cause despair' to his producer (Bill Duncalf of course, for Kelly now would have no one else). The *Daily Sketch* noted that he tended to ignore the microphones that surrounded him and to face the wrong way. Twice he asked 'How much more time have I got?' – to be answered by a disembodied voice. Once he gave away the secret signals by crying sharply, 'What's the matter?'

A nagging conscience still drew him back to his first sensational performance of two years earlier.

> I was ashamed, I lost my temper, I waved my hands, I swore, and the funny thing is that it worked. You all forgave me because I had not intended to do it. Rembrandt's picture reduced me to impotent swearing. (*The Daily Telegraph* report.)

And when he came to a still-life by Melendez, about which he had enthused to Miss Hubbard in one of his letters from Paris, he allowed a glimpse of his unregenerate self: 'I assure you, as in Paradise I hope to clean Velasquez' brushes, that this is a blank masterpiece.'

The famous Boucher nude of a girl lying face downwards inspired the comment:

> Now this is lyrical, light, and superficial. If you insist on your pictures having a high moral content, then this is not your picture. But if you want beauty and grace, then here you are. You can't see what she has in front . . . but you can see what she has behind. (*Daily Express* report.)

His conclusion was characteristically quirky: 'This is the last time I shall be speaking to you in the Royal Academy. I wish you well, but I wish myself much better. Good night.'

Writing in *The Listener* (3 February 1955), Reginald Pound said that as an art popularizer Kelly was 'entertainingly persuasive, with a liveliness of spirit alien to all official gallery guides,' and he continued:

> His enthusiasms lose nothing with the years, and on Friday night he fairly bounced us into sharing his raptures about Watteau's 'nice conduct' of a dainty hand and Chardin's way with candlesticks. For him art is joy . . . We viewers can but hope that the note of finality which he sounded in his talk on Friday night will be heard, *prima donna* fashion, again and yet again. B.B.C. television cannot afford to part with Sir Gerald. . . .

The B.B.C. had no intention of parting with their discovery, whom, indeed, they eventually put on a year's contract. Nor was this the last time Kelly was to speak to viewers from Burlington House.

6

In retrospect it can be seen that Kelly's five years as President revitalized the Royal Academy. The exhibitions assembled under his leadership were outstanding, and he adapted the Diploma Gallery to increase their scope. His enterprise and skill in persuading owners at home and abroad to part with their treasures resulted in superb displays which gave tremendous pleasure.

On the other hand, Kelly's critics have maintained that his exhibitions were too large and inadequately organized; that they skimmed the cream of pictures and good will, so that after his time the Academy found it increasingly hard, in a period of continual inflation, to keep the pace going.

With hindsight, some of this criticism may be justified, but it cannot upset Clive Bell's assertion that Kelly was 'about the best president the Royal Academy has given itself since Sir Joshua Reynolds'. A flash of lightning in the darkness 'coineth the mind with that scene sharper than fifty summers'. And glancing down the list of Presidents of the Royal Academy we do not again find Kelly's combination of Churchillian energy with informed intelligence.

To compare him with an historical figure like Sir Joshua Reynolds might be misleading. 'There lives our friend,' said Boswell to Dr Johnson as they passed Reynolds' house: 'Ay, Sir,' replied Johnson, 'there lives a very great man.' But it is worth mentioning that Reynolds died at the age of 68, having been P.R.A. for 23 years; Kelly was already 70 when he began his five-year period of office.

This argues for vitality of an exceptional kind – as does the fact that Kelly became better known to the general public than any other President before or since. Sir Joshua was not cut out for television. With his deafness, poor eyesight, and indistinct speech, Reynolds and his ear-trumpet would have given more trouble to a B.B.C. producer than ever Gerald Kelly did.

CHAPTER THIRTEEN

House and Home

I

With Kelly's retirement from the Presidency of the Royal Academy – he was invested as K.C.V.O. in 1955 – peace descended on the official side of his activity; telephones rang less frequently; fewer letters and telegrams came from all over the world ('URGENTE SIR KELLY PRESIDENTE ROYAL ACADEMY ARTS'). But he was still often to be seen at Burlington House. He remained President of the Reynolds Club, an association of old R.A. students formed in November 1951. Kelly was their president from the beginning; he attended seven annual dinners and gave an amusing speech at each of them.

After a trip to Italy with Sir Owen Morshead in September 1955, Kelly was thrown into a struggle to save his home in Gloucester Place, where he had lived for forty years. The lease was about to expire, and the house formed part of the Portman Estate which had been sold to meet death duties. There was a time when Kelly could have bought the house for a reasonable sum; having missed that chance, he had to pay much more. The journalists who now pursued him at every opportunity found Kelly willing to discuss his predicament. He explained that he was having to part with many of his personal treasures. These included fine Empire furniture inherited from his father; Chinese bronzes and pottery; a small bronze which Rodin had given him; Spanish wood-carvings; drawings by Aubrey Beardsley; valuable books.

'We have to buy the house or move,' Kelly told *The Daily Telegraph*. 'When you get to my age, you don't want all these possessions around. When we first lived here we had five servants. Now that is out of the question. We live here like two dried peas in a pod.'

All the same, it was a great wrench to have to sell the unique series of first editions, proofs, and manuscript material which Somerset

Maugham had given him over the years. He consulted Maugham – and of course was told to go ahead.

At the beginning of November, furniture and works of art, in 34 lots, were sold at Sotheby's for £1,277 (*The Times*, 5 November 1955); there was a further sale on 18 November of furniture and several lots of Spanish wood-carvings. The books were sold at Sotheby's on 7 December, among them rare publications from the Ashendene, Doves, Kelmscott, Nonesuch, and Vale Presses, and first editions of modern writers, including some of Hugh Walpole's with friendly inscriptions by their author.

The Maugham collection formed an almost complete set of his books and plays. It included a copy of the first edition of *Liza of Lambeth* (1897): 'For Gerald. W. Somerset Maugham. My first book.' *The Explorer* (1908) was dismissed in the author's inscription as 'his worst book'. A first edition of *Of Human Bondage* (1915) was offered to 'Gerald Kelly A.R.A. from William Somerset Maugham M.R.C.S., L.R.C.P.' A copy of the first issue of the first edition of *The Painted Veil* (1925) contained Maugham's comment that it had been 'withdrawn on the eve of publication because the Assistant Colonial Secretary at Hong-Kong threatened to bring an action for libel' and that 'the name of the Colony was changed to an imaginary one'. *Cakes and Ale* (1930) was 'a very innocent book' and *Sheppey* (1933) 'the author's last play'. The collection included three proofs of the first edition of *The Summing Up* (1938) with Maugham's own corrections. *The Vagrant Mood* (1952) was inscribed 'For Gerald P.R.A. from his old, old friend. Willie.'

The most interesting item was the original manuscript of *The Moon and Sixpence*, the novel based on Gauguin's life. Sotheby's catalogue carried a note saying that in 1903 Maugham and Kelly together visited the famous exhibition at the Galérie Vollard in Paris which established Gauguin's reputation.

All these sacrifices helped Kelly to keep his house. The top floor was turned into a separate flat. The large front-door was divided into two, and from the second entrance a special staircase for the tenants led upwards. It was an ingenious and successful scheme.

2

One of Kelly's continuing worries in his seventies was that there were far too many art students in Britain. While still P.R.A., and also President of the Artists' General Benevolent Institution, he had spoken at the annual meeting of the latter body of the 'rather gloomy future' in the world of art, and said this was because modern painting could be done easily and there were a great many people doing it: 'I am quite frankly haunted by the idea that there will be a terrible increase of unsuccessful painters who will in future look to the Institution for help.' (*The Times*, 28 October 1954.)

He revived the theme a year later in a presidential address to Smethwick Society of Arts, urging parents to be stern with their children when they 'babbled' about going in for the fine arts. 'They are going to have a grim time,' he said:

> Even if the little blighters have any ability, what chance do they have? They have been taught by teachers who cannot perform themselves; 120,000 art students have been processed since the war in the mesh of art instruction which lies over the country . . . It does seem rum to me that we have all these art students in a country which, in the past, has not produced many good painters. I am frightened about what is coming to the young. Modern painting has got into a frightful mess. There is too much teaching and too much encouragement going on. (*The Times*, 12 October 1955.)

The chaotic happenings at art schools in the next twenty years have justified Kelly's attitude on this question. But in general he was not primarily concerned to utter warnings, but to convey some of his own unflagging zest for great art to the widest possible audience. He made many converts through television, and soon found an opportunity of advertising his beloved Dulwich Gallery. 'Did Anybody *Not* See Kelly?' ran a headline in the *Daily Herald* (23 November 1955) after his television tour of the Dulwich pictures the night before. The critic of the *Star* said his return to television was 'like a breath of pure oxygen to a rush hour tube traveller' and continued:

> He called himself 'one derelict past president of the Royal Academy, withered, grey, worn out, and on the shelf.' But a few million viewers, I am sure, are going to insist that he come off it. He was modest about his own achievements with a brush. But with his personality he painted some brilliant pictures on our screens. He apologized for talking too much – 'I always do.' But talk on, Sir Gerald. We'll be listening.

Peter Black in the *Daily Mail* said he couldn't imagine Kelly being 'less than a smash hit' on television. He compared him to a literary painter who might have been invented by Dickens. He thought him 'a born talker, with a striking gift for vivid imagery, a power to communicate enthusiasm; a full man who speaks out of what he suggests as being a happy, satisfying life'.

Whatever the B.B.C. paid for Kelly's twelve-month contract, 'it was worth it', thought the *Herald*. If the autobiographical element did become dominant, the uninhibited Kelly was gratefully accepted by a vast majority of his viewers. Describing early visits to Dulwich as a child with his governess Miss Bird, he said that when he insisted on standing on his head, she had grabbed him by the ankles and swung him like a golf-club. He called himself 'a wicked old man', who had 'constantly eaten too much, drunk too much, and broken every law with a careful eye on the policeman round the corner' (the last words were a quotation from Somerset Maugham). He talked of the love affairs of his youth; his 'Frankly Speaking' radio interview of 1953 had already revealed his preference in women; it was for those with 'small noses and big mouths – rather like King Charles's spaniels – Renoir painted my best girl over and over again – Aquiline noses, no good to me! . . . But give me something not much bigger than a button. . . .' (Lady Kelly found this curious, as her own nose was planned on a slightly more generous scale.)

Poussin's odd picture 'The Nurture of Jupiter' at Dulwich had a lasting fascination for Kelly. It shows a muscular young man holding the horns of a puzzled goat so that it can suckle a lusty infant. The goat's left leg is firmly restrained by a statuesque beauty – perhaps one of the topless Miss Towers of Ilium. When Gerald came to the gallery at the age of eleven, he said to Miss Bird, 'That's very peculiar'; and she looked at him and said, 'You know, it very rarely happens. I shouldn't worry.' On this television programme he drew attention to another feature of the Poussin – a young nymph taking a swarm of bees, 'and she has no protection against them – why they're not giving her hell I don't know'.

3

Not surprisingly, the B.B.C. saw great television possibilities in Kelly's reminiscences. A series of six programmes, 'Sir Gerald Kelly Remembers', was now planned by him and Bill Duncalf over the bare white-scrubbed table in the kitchen at Gloucester Place, where Jane prepared delicious meals for them and they drank vintage wine from the cellar. Gerald assembled his thoughts; in talking, he used no notes but he was mentally prepared for the cameras when they moved into his studio. There, surrounded by the paraphernalia of his craft – canvases on easels and canvases in racks, the air scented by linseed oil and turpentine – he sat in his painting overall, and just talked. He talked, in fact, for thousands more feet of film than the B.B.C. could show.

Up to a point, this was deliberate policy. Duncalf wisely treated the production as a live broadcast and allowed Kelly to correct himself and occasionally fumble his words. The result was natural, affectionate, vivid. Six programmes were broadcast in the Spring of 1956: one called 'Early Days', one on Monet, two on Rodin, and the others on Maillol and Cézanne. Material from the talks has been used in the opening chapters of this book. They were a great success, and several were put out again a year later.

There were no sensational outbursts – a few contentious remarks were edited away, but Kelly had now acquired restraint without losing magnetism. 'In the sea of TV sameness, this series, *Sir Gerald Kelly Remembers*, is conspicuous because it reflects unusual qualities and character,' said *The Daily Telegraph* (23 April 1956).

When it came to cutting the film, Kelly had been hard to please. He insisted, understandably, that he should be consulted; but perhaps failed to appreciate a producer's difficulties. 'It is ridiculous to cut it down making nonsense of some of the sentences,' he complained in one letter to the B.B.C., 'and at the same time introduce such a foolish interpolation as to show an old steel engraving of Trinity in order to point the fact that I went to Trinity Hall.'

He complained, too, that the ending of his second talk on Rodin had been spoiled, and feared that his 'characteristics' might be 'whittled away'. 'The best one,' maintained Kelly, 'is a very Irish trick of suddenly being all sentimental.' He succeeded in having the original ending restored, and this is how his last recollection of Rodin reads:

. . . We went back to the studio, and he showed me what he was working on, and then I said 'May I look at the hands?' And this, I think, is worth telling you about. When he was a young man he used to model a hand, quite small, half the size of life, little things, that sort of size, little hands, and he never threw one away, he kept clay squeezes of them and they were arranged in drawers, shallow drawers, about that wide, which wanted very carefully opening so that they didn't stick, and there were all these little tiny hands, and I loved looking at them. And he showed me the hands and we picked out one or two that were particularly good, and I remember him with one little hand in each of his, smiling, and saying 'How good they are.' That is how I remember Rodin and I remember his kissing the horse's nose in the British Museum.*

(B.B.C. transcript.)

The transcripts of those filmed recollections that were discarded suggest that the B.B.C. did a good job in preparing the six programmes actually broadcast. It is true that intriguing fragments were lost to television, including glimpses of Degas and Sarah Bernhardt, but something had to go, and Kelly did become rather emotional in looking back fifty years to his Paris days.

As mentioned in Chapter 3, the actress Marguerite Moréno once sternly rebuked the young Gerald for not having the slightest idea of what had been happening in a Russian play performed by Duse. She said he was 'insincere, a snob and a rotter'! Gerald had wept. But then Sarah Bernhardt came in, to tell Marguerite Moréno that a rehearsal date had been changed, and Kelly met for the first time 'the woman I most admired in the world'. The story, as Kelly told it before the television cameras, aged 77, may be continued (though the film was never used):

> . . . Madame Sarah looked at me, and she said 'What's that . . .?' And there was I, flushed, a bit red in the nose, a bit watery in the eye, not looking my best. And Marguerite started straight off and told her the whole story and she piled it up, all about the insincerity, and Sarah was looking at me. I didn't care a damn about what I had done, I was actually staring at her, after all, I mean, it was Sarah, and she stared at me, and then she winked. The smallest, plumpest, kindest little wink that ever was wunk. I recognized that she understood and it made a very, very great difference. (B.B.C. transcript.)

Thinking of this lachrymose episode, and remembering the great Sarah, set Kelly off again and he wept once more – this time before the television cameras, which was probably one reason why that piece of film was never broadcast. However, a divine wink has at least been retrieved from the cutting-room floor.

* See p. 16.

4

Although Kelly's passion for great painting was the central motive of his life, he had a great love for the stage – and also for the ballet, which stemmed from his memories of Nijinsky and Pavlova, and of the early performances of the Russian Ballet which he saw in Paris. In 1954 he accepted an invitation to become a member of the Grand Council of the Royal Academy of Dancing and one of the judges for a Coronation award presented by Dame Adeline Genée. This entailed an address to the Academy of Dancing, which Kelly delivered in July 1956. As soon as he had given it, he wrote characteristically to Dame Margot Fonteyn, the President, to apologize for its deficiencies (23 July 1956):

> I am so glad that awful speech is over. I am richly endowed with what the French call *l'esprit d'escalier* and I have been improving that speech in my mind ever since I stopped.
>
> I did intend but unfortunately forgot to address myself more noticeably to the teachers and categorically to tell them how essential teachers are to any craft and how valuable. I also intended to say that you had told me that most of the audience were teachers and one of them a few years ago had given lessons to a little girl of five. But like an ass I forgot. I am sure your teacher would have liked it had I said it and I intended to say it to please you. . . .

Dame Margot's reply swiftly reassured him that he had not lost his power to hold and delight an audience, especially one consisting principally of the opposite sex:

> 17a Thurloe Place,
> S.W.7.
> 25th July

Dear Sir Gerald,

It is quite typical of my general inefficiency that this thank-you letter should not be written until after I had received a most charming letter from you about Friday afternoon's meeting.

I simply cannot tell you how much your address was appreciated and enjoyed by all present. As you saw there were many students as well as teachers. Your reminiscences touched on people that were present and people that many of us were never fortunate enough to see. For the members of an Academic institution it is so important to have the inspiration of an eminent 'outsider's' interest and appreciation. That is what makes all the routine classwork have some meaning and object. Your address was absolutely right and everything it should have been. Goodness knows how you were able to do it at such short notice. Many people have told me how much they enjoyed it, including Dame Adeline who wrote me a letter about it.

Incidentally the choice of Mme Rambert for the award seems to have been approved enthusiastically by all quarters.

Again my most heartfelt thanks to you.

Yours sincerely,

MARGOT ARIAS.

CHAPTER FOURTEEN

An Indomitable Painter

I

For several more years the B.B.C. kept Kelly busy on television (and also to some extent on sound radio). In November 1956, he made a television tour of the Wallace Collection with Sir James Mann, the Director, and (Sir) Francis Watson, Mann's eventual successor. Kelly was a close friend of Watson, who had helped him greatly with the European eighteenth-century exhibition at Burlington House. In May 1957, there was another television appearance from Dulwich, and in April 1958 Kelly introduced viewers to the collection at Kenwood. During the late nineteen-fifties he appeared in panel games – 'Animal, Vegetable, Mineral?' and 'Who Said That?' – and in two series called 'Masterpieces of Painting' and 'Masters of Portraiture'.

Kelly had come to enjoy his television performances and was full of ideas for continuing them; but inevitably the time arrived when a new generation in authority at the B.B.C. grew less enthusiastic about him than its predecessors. Sensing this, Kelly discussed the problem with Reginald Pound, who was at one time his neighbour in Welbeck Street. 'In the past the B.B.C. used to run after me and it was all very pleasant,' he wrote to Pound on 27 September 1961; 'if I force my way into their programmes . . . will the atmosphere be as jolly as it used to be?'

This rhetorical question cannot be fairly answered, as Kelly was anyway close to the end of his television career. He showed, however, that he had not lost his Pied Piper touch when – at the age of nearly 85 – he televised the Goya exhibition at the Royal Academy in 1964. He was then recorded for the first time on video magnetic tape (22 January), to be broadcast a fortnight later. With Bill Duncalf, Humphrey Brooke, and Innes Lloyd, who directed the programme, Kelly sat down to his favourite snack, a caviare and vodka supper, before the recording. After the actual broadcast, the daily attendance figures for the Goya exhibition immediately trebled to over 8,000.

2

One engagement Kelly never expected to undertake was a television tour of his own retrospective exhibition, held in the Diploma Gallery of the Royal Academy in the autumn of 1957. But in fact he took Bill Duncalf round the show on 31 October, and the following day's *Evening Standard* had the headline 'Not a Naughty Word from Sir Gerald'.

Kelly contributed this note to the catalogue:

> When I was President I persuaded the Council to agree to hold an exhibition of Sir Frank Brangwyn's pictures and drawings, though he was still alive. I argued that the old system of holding exhibitions after the painter was dead could give him no satisfaction and the works weren't always wisely chosen. For instance, the wonderful exhibition of John S. Sargent wouldn't have been so much too big if that modest man had been allowed a say in the matter. And I remember the McEvoys, so many of which I don't believe for a moment he himself would have chosen.
>
> After Brangwyn came the Augustus John Exhibition, and then my successor continued with Munnings.
>
> I never dreamed that I should be invited here also. And, indeed, when it was first suggested I quickly refused because I felt that I wasn't good enough. I thought the Academy had invited me because I had been a useful President rather than because I was a good painter.
>
> But to my surprise, after a little while, the Council repeated the invitation and this time my vanity swept away my common sense and good judgement.
>
> Well, here is the best we could do about it. My friends have hung the exhibition beautifully. Make what you can of it, I can do no more.

Fifty of Kelly's paintings had been exhibited at the Leicester Galleries in 1950; nearly three hundred of his works were now gathered together at Burlington House. Henry Rushbury and Edward Le Bas helped Kelly to select and arrange them. Sir Charles Wheeler, P.R.A., contributed a graceful preface to the catalogue, in which he said it was 'particularly apt that Sir Gerald Kelly should be the fourth Member of the Royal Academy to be honoured in his lifetime with a retrospective Exhibition, for it was under his memorable Presidency, and in no small measure due to his imagination, that the Diploma Gallery was first brought into use for special Exhibitions of this kind'. He went on to deprecate Kelly's undue modesty as a painter and his tendency to regard himself 'as a craftsman with no loftier pretension than that of taking infinite trouble over the task in hand'. Wheeler emphasized the 'skill and penetration' of his portraits, instancing the early portraits of his father and Mrs Harrison, and he added: 'One notices the almost fault-less state of his canvases, a test of expert technique and of trouble taken, in the tradition of the meticulous masters of the past.'

The versatility of Kelly's display surprised the sceptics who thought of him only as a fastidious portrait-painter. That element certainly predominated – and had historical advantages for an exhibition which included the State Portraits of King George VI and Queen Elizabeth (as well as several lively sketches for these) and a gallery of contrasting portraits of the famous from Lady Gregory, Kay Francis, and Marie Stopes, to Ralph Vaughan Williams, Sir Malcolm Sargent, and Sir Almroth Wright. There were, naturally, a number of delightful por-traits of Jane – whom, according to Sir Charles Wheeler, Kelly had attempted to paint more than ninety times – and several likenesses of his oldest friend Somerset Maugham. But Kelly's worldwide travels gave the exhibition an unexpected colour and richness. Although the landscapes and figure studies of 1902–14 were often painted in France, Spain, or Burma, there were, even from these years, pictures of 'The Beach at Eastbourne' or 'Kennington Oval' to assert English loyalties and remind the visitor that Kelly would happily set up his easel before any paintable subject, wherever he happened to be. Many of his *pochades* could now be seen to have a lasting attraction. If this was hardly true of 'The Sphinx', which the Academy had asked to be excused from ex-hibiting in 1930, that large nude study was nevertheless an unsparing tour-de-force.

The critic of *The Times* (11 October 1957) thought Kelly's work filled the four rooms of the Diploma Gallery 'remarkably well':

. . . A Kelly portrait in the crowded and often clamorous sur-roundings of a Summer Exhibition at the Academy can look rather too cool and patiently literal to be altogether likeable. Here the variety of his sitters and the artist's commendably consistent level of achievement in doing the best he can by each of them while effacing everything of himself except his good taste can be appreciated rather differently. His industry, his craftsmanship, and his unexceptionable accomplishment as a literal draughtsman are the most honest of virtues.

The critics agreed in finding that Kelly's portraits painted before 1914 often had a human warmth, and sometimes a lyric poetry, that was rare in his later work. John Russell asked the pertinent question:

> Where did this poet go to? Did somebody sit on his head? Perhaps some notion of painterly 'good form' was the assassin?
> It is a curious fact, in any case, that Sir Gerald's style has varied hardly at all in the last forty years, and his habit of worrying and re-worrying a picture never results in incongruity of manner. Public life and the flashing phrase have drained off, perhaps, the wildness that might have gone into the pictures. (*The Sunday Times*, 13 October 1957.)

In *The Observer* of the same date, Nevile Wallis pointed out that no recent President had tried harder than Kelly to rally public confidence in the Royal Academy, and he asked who could have foretold that 'the young Irish painter of sensibility' would emerge in this role. 'One is conscious of an agile, baffling little figure,' wrote Wallis, 'which might pass (like Max's T. Fenning Dodworth) for a statuette of Seneca, and has become, through the magic lantern, a household image.'

Kelly's character undoubtedly held a baffling element for many. As John Russell maintained, the mystery centred in the contrast 'between his easy and flexible approach, in life, to his fellow human beings and the long agony of exactitude with which he addresses himself to his canvas.' The volatile artist son of an Irish clergyman in the Church of England might be expected to show complexities; yet the biographical facts are simple; on his very happy marriage at the age of forty-one, Kelly abandoned the Bohemian life and settled down. His own art may have suffered, but his craftsmanship did not falter; paradoxically, art in general and its public appreciation gained immeasurably.

3

When Kelly's Academy exhibition closed, selections of his pictures were sent by the Art Exhibitions Bureau on tours of the country lasting several years. The first of these local exhibitions was held at the

Ferens Art Gallery, Hull. In opening it, Kelly – who called himself 'this curious old man' – took the opportunity to re-emphasize his views on art education, and to stress the importance of allowing the young to make up their own minds. True culture, he said, was what we really believed, not what a group of experts thought it was good for us to believe. Referring to his own early dislike of Rembrandt's work, he continued:

> Do you think an intelligent, successful young man of seventeen today can afford to say he does not like Bach or Rembrandt? Of course he cannot.
>
> If you have children, encourage them not to read anything about art at all. Music is to be listened to, art and sculpture are to be looked at. Don't bring your intellect into play. Use it as a super-exquisite instrument which can be carefully and gradually applied as you grow older.
>
> Fashion is all right; you cannot escape it – it is like the weather. But if you are to get real satisfaction – profound emotional, deep satisfaction – you must start by being wrong and correct your own fashion. (*Hull Daily Mail*, 2 April 1958.)

Soon after this speech at Hull, Kelly entered on a sequence of illnesses and misfortunes, during which he was unable to paint for long periods. The first enemy was neuralgia; throughout the summer of 1958 he was in constant pain. On 18 December 1958, he wrote to Sir Owen Morshead from 117 Gloucester Place:

> I had 5 months of pain increasing, unbearable.
>
> A great neurologist identified neuralgia of the glossopharyngeal nerve & on Wed 19th Nov. I was operated on. On Sunday 30th I was returned here. In short tho' 79½ yrs old I had behaved admirably. My surgeon thought as highly of me as I did of him.
>
> *And no more pain*
> *nor fear of pain.*
> *Wonderful.*

Unfortunately, though the major operation by Wylie McKissock was a complete success, the pains returned at the end of January 1959, and were very bad until April, when they gradually faded. Gerald and Jane then went to Spain for a holiday. Soon after their return, Sir Alfred Munnings died, and Lionel Edwards – another fine painter of horses – wrote to Kelly protesting at the tone of a newspaper comment on his death. Kelly's reply to Edwards (21 July 1959) contains an appreciation of his predecessor as P.R.A., whose better qualities he had never ceased to admire:

I've read your little letter (with the grudging, smeary little press-cutting), and I thank you for the generous indignation which inspired it.

I did write a little about A.J. in *The Sunday Times*. I was told that he had died in his sleep, I had seen his crumpled hands which could not hold a brush, and they had told me how he admitted he longed to die. Physical disabilities make old age a horrible thing so I was glad to hear of his death.

I think one can safely admit that he over-produced. I do not like the fashionable people on their rich horses, but every now and then, into the most commonplace of these compositions, there will come a passage of paint so exquisitely right. I wonder whether you saw a one-man show he gave in the Leicester Galleries I think in 1949 which mainly consisted of small pictures about 20″ × 18″, and they were tender, pearly-grey in colour with the jockeys in their bright colours. I saw it with a friend and we were rapt by the beauty of them, and I said to one of the people in the Gallery that I wished Degas was not dead for I would have loved to pop over to Paris with half a dozen, and show them to him. He would have liked them. Munnings was a much better artist than people thought, who could only jealously regard the ease with which he earned such considerable sums of money.

That grudging, smearing notice: Don't get too angry with what art critics and art boys say. They are a wretched lot, but remember what that disagreeable but intelligent man Jules Renard said of critics: 'Poor fellows, they are always writing about other people and nobody ever writes about them.'

I have just returned from Spain where my wife and I sat in front of the Meninas* (which is a greater thing than Munnings ever painted) and occasionally we watched people looking at it. Few people looked at it for as much as half a minute. We spent a long time in front of it day after day for a fortnight, and I have spent hours and hours in the old days in front of it, but I have never noticed anybody looking at that picture for as much as five minutes.

Sir John Rothenstein, with whom I do not often agree, told me

* 'Las Meninas' by Velasquez, in the Prado at Madrid.

Kelly with Sir Owen Morshead, May 1953, preparing to conduct B.B.C. viewers round the special 'Kings and Queens' exhibition collected in the Diploma Galleries of the Royal Academy to mark the coronation (B.B.C. copyright photograph).

Sir Alfred Munnings, Sir Gerald Kelly and Sir Albert Richardson toast the new P.R.A., Sir Charles Wheeler, 11 December 1956.

Kelly's studio at 117 Gloucester Place, London W.1.

that nobody looks at pictures to observe what is there. They come in with ready-made blame or ready-made praise. Rather let us thank the Gods that we are painters, we have had the fun of doing it, which is so much greater than the disappointment of finding out it is not as good as one hoped, and we have been able to get so much pleasure out of Munnings' so many and such lovely paintings.

I myself believe that the best of his pictures will be treasured when modern cerebral productions have been relegated to another place.

4

The mishaps that continued to befall Kelly at eighty might be compared to the sufferings of Job or the sad tidings brought by a messenger in a Greek play. He kept Morshead up to date in a letter of 22 December 1959:

> . . . On October 17th, I fell heavily in the kitchen and subsequently it turned out that I had broken a blood vessel, but without even cracking the thigh bone. This entailed several weeks of very bad pain, however I got over it all right and was just about cured when on November 30th, I was knocked down by a van. My glasses were smashed, umbrella smashed and left humerus broken 2″ below the level of the shoulder. Fortunately all this occurred barely 40 yards from the front door of the Orthopaedic Hospital, so that within a few minutes, I was back there, warmed, X-rayed and strapped up and safely in bed.
>
> My surgeon, Mr Manning, assures me that if I obey his instructions he can guarantee a clean mend. So for 22 days I have been doing that and I think he is satisfied with me, except that I have caught the most frightful cold and have spent ten days in bed.
>
> It sounds bloody, doesn't it, Owen? Such a waste of time, but I still feel that I have plenty of energy and if these accidents would only stop, I could go back to the workshop and paint with the usual pleasure.
>
> This is the best time of the year for a painter to be ill, since there is so little day-light.

Such determination was bound to prevail. Kelly eventually got back to his studio – and to the daily round of secretaries and sitters. In the

late summer of 1960, he engaged a new secretary, Penelope Mackay
(later Mrs Reid), who vividly remembers the two years she spent with
him:

> My first sight of my future boss was appropriately and happily
> enough at his easel in the huge studio. We shook hands and looked
> each other in the eye, seemingly; I am five foot four but I expect I
> wore stiletto heels, for this was 1960. Anyway I was immensely
> impressed; although I had landed the interview on the reputation
> of being artistic, this was a far cry from the Art Wing of Chelten-
> ham Ladies College.
>
> The artist was at work in a blue boiler suit *au Churchill* and he
> had a really sharp pair of eyes behind bifocal glasses.
>
> 'How old are you?' he said.
>
> 'Nineteen,' I replied.
>
> 'I'm eighty-one, God help us both.'
>
> I got the job.

An average day's work began when Miss Mackay arrived at Gloucester
Place at ten o'clock. Kelly came down to breakfast about the same
time. His secretary would grab her shorthand pad and pencil, and
clatter down the stone stairs into the basement, where Lady Kelly had
her all-purpose kitchen-dining room, with a huge range, a scrubbed
pine table, and a dresser set with china. 'It was all very practical and
cosy,' thought Miss Mackay; and she continues:

> Lady Kelly would have breakfasted by this time but Sir Gerald
> was usually just shaved, white hair brushed, and already boiler-
> suited for the day's work. There was a marvellous French earthen-
> ware pot of *filtre* coffee and hot milk for us both, and I would put
> an egg in to boil and make a couple of slices of toast. Letters would
> be opened and I would take dictation. Not very much by normal
> commercial standards but there was a fairly esoteric vocabulary to
> acquire. However, the content of the correspondence was on the
> whole so very much more interesting than my secretarial training
> could have led me to expect. Someone of eighty, still vital in mind
> and body, who had combined an upper-class English background
> and education with an abiding passion for and knowledge of
> painting provided a nineteen-year-old intellectual *manqué* with
> much food for thought. So my main impression of my time with
> Sir Gerald is of acquiring information and education. He was an
> extrovert and far from discreet, I suppose. I would lap up gossip

from past and present, and much of Sir Gerald's life had been distinctly romantic, after all. I can't remember whether I read *Trilby* before or after this time, but certainly the life in Paris he described conjured up the whole uninhibited, vastly creative, bohemian thing.

I can remember him saying about a painting, a Japanese print, a bottle of wine – and it applies to anything created by man – 'This is right.' The word 'right' seems to me now highly significant when I think of Sir Gerald. He couldn't abide fake, or humbug, or lack of integrity. I think this is an instinct which he nurtured in me also. 'It's not right' – this was his strongest term of opprobrium.

Among Kelly's sitters in 1960–62 were Sir Cyril Hinshelwood, Somerset Maugham, and T. S. Eliot and his second wife. The painting of Mr and Mrs Eliot's portraits, though eventually successfully completed, was delayed by another misfortune for Kelly – 'an attack of sciatica of the utmost virulence' on Christmas Eve, 1960. Kelly described what followed in a letter to Sir Owen Morshead (14 April 1961):

> . . . They took me into the Royal National Orthopaedic Hospital, cured me in a fortnight, and then there started a series of attacks by some form of rheumatism. I had no idea that a stiff neck could be so painful but at long last, having ruined the last six months of my life as far as painting is concerned, my surgeon and my doctor agree that I am going to get through all right and though at present my neck is supported by an artificial contraption, it does seem as though I shall get better. It may be a fortnight hence, three months, or even a little longer, but I am promised a complete cure.

Eliot had been away from London. He hastened to express sympathy as soon as he heard of the setback for his indomitable painter:

London W.8.
8 April, 1961

My dear Gerald Kelly,

We were on the point of apprising you of our return (having dealt with the numerous immediate claims that are inevitable after such a long absence) when your letter of the 5th, with its dolorous news, arrived. We are distressed by the report of a winter spent in pain – and suffering which has imposed abeyance of work. We do pray for a speedy recovery. We may be out of

London during much of June, but on the whole we are at your disposal until (probably) October.

It will be good news of your restoration to health when you summon us again.

With most cordial greetings from both of us to both of you.

Yours ever,

TOM ELIOT.

Your writing is as beautiful as ever.

P.S. My wife says to me: 'The nicest thing that has happened to me since marrying you is being invited by Gerald Kelly to sit to him.'

The Eliots were visitors in Gloucester Place over several years. Kelly showed portraits of the poet at the Academy in 1962, 1965 and 1969. Eliot was particularly delighted with the first of these (Plate 9b):

London W.8.

29th July, 1962

Dear Gerald,

Of course we will be sitting again, just as soon as we have got straight after three weeks' absence and a fresh inroad of American visitors.

But meanwhile I want to arrive at an agreement with you about my portrait which has been shown at the Academy this year. This is a masterpiece and I shall never have a better portrait even from yourself. Valerie wants it, and I want her to have it. So here is my cheque . . . This I offer with the following stipulations:

1. That you don't touch the head and face
   again. The face is so good that it cannot
   be improved. Remember the moral of
   Balzac's *Chef d'oeuvre inconnu*.
2. That we have it when this Academy show closes
   in August. We would be willing to lend it
   out for some important show of your work later,
   but we want to see it on our wall first before
   it tours the country.

Our love to you both,

Yours affectionately,

TOM.

5

Although Kelly could not spend so much time in his studio as formerly, there was one picture he was determined to paint, without thought of financial reward, and that was a full-size seated portrait of Sir Owen Morshead. Kelly still required an exacting number of sittings. He did not spare his old friend in this respect. The bitter winter of 1962–3 was memorable for Morshead because he travelled up to London in cold trains to sit for Kelly fifteen times. But Morshead thought it extraordinarily generous when his portrait was presented to him, beautifully framed, for his seventieth birthday. It was shown in the 1963 Academy.

The instinct for making his own life and those of others happier and more interesting persisted into Kelly's old age, and flourished after he had shed official cares and frustrations.

Being sometimes confined to his home, he took increasing pleasure in music. His collection of gramophone records gave him much enjoyment; he also listened to music on the radio. After winning the first competition in the B.B.C.'s 'Let the People Sing' programme for schools, the choir of Kendal High School broadcast several times. They posed a problem which Kelly was determined to solve:

> 117 Gloucester Place,
> Portman Square, W.1.
> 25th September, 1961

Madame,

I know you exist because I heard you speak. Last Sunday at five o'clock as I listened to 'Places Where they Sing' I heard the choir of Kendal High School and the producer of the programme spoke to you.

During this, your small singers gave a performance of a song and the confounded thing has got into my mind and ruined my peace. I cannot hum it and when I whistle it the noises I make are not the notes I want. It was a soft, gay, sweet little tune which went on, and as it finished it began again, like bits of Mozart.

What is the name of the beastly but charming thing and is there a record of your children singing it?

They won some competition. Help me if you can recognize what I'm talking about.

GERALD KELLY.

The Choir Mistress,
Kendal High School,
Kendal, Westmorland.

The Choir Mistress was Margaret Hine, who promptly responded by sending Kelly the music of 'The Prickety Bush', a folk song attractively arranged by Francis Collinson, which she rightly believed was the tune that had got into Kelly's head.

29th September, 1961

Dear Miss Margaret Hine,

Thank you for your kind letter and the gift of 'The Prickety Bush'.

The only one of my friends who plays the piano (and he plays a very pretty piano) is Sir Malcolm Sargent, so when he returns from the north of Italy I will try and get him to play this tune to me and I will see if you have guessed right. I can't play, not even with one finger, but occasionally I buy a record and if 'The Prickety Bush' is my tune I should like to get a record of your children singing it.

Thanks a lot.

GERALD KELLY.

30th November, 1961

Dear Miss Margaret Hine,

How very nice of you to send me the tape recording of your children singing 'The Prickety Bush'. I am having arrangements made for it to be played to me and when I have heard it I shall write to thank you more fully.

Yours sincerely,

GERALD KELLY.

1st December, 1961

Dear Miss Margaret Hine,

You really have been kind to me.

This morning I managed to get a machine to play the recording of 'The Prickety Bush' and I loved it.

I have given Malcolm Sargent the printed sheet with the words which you kindly sent me but I must get him to give it back to me because I cannot make out all of the words. But it is an enchanting thing and there is nothing to beat what my friend calls 'the freshness of youthful voices'. They sing charmingly; you have given me immense pleasure.

If you have any other recordings of your singers, let me know as I should *like to buy them*.

Your grateful admirer,

GERALD KELLY.

In 1964 Miss Hine was able to send Kelly a private record of songs sung by her choir – which included their rendering of 'The Prickety Bush'.

18th June, 1964

Dear Margaret Hine,

How very kind of you; how very, very kind. We played your record through last night and it is charming. I know that I shall play it over and over again in the years to come.

What fun it is for the children – (I do not know how old they are even) – and what fun it must be to sing such lovely things and so well. You must enjoy it all too.

If you come from Kendal to London one of these days, please come and see me. I should like to thank you in person.

I still play your 'Prickety Bush' and it still gives me *great* pleasure.

Yours,

GERALD KELLY.

When Miss Hine and her sister next visited London, they telephoned Kelly and were invited to call the same day, a Sunday. 'Sir Gerald spent quite a long time with us,' writes Margaret Hine, 'telling us of his earlier life, and showed us his studio and many of his pictures. He was most gracious and we thoroughly enjoyed our time with him.'

6

If there were now, in the nineteen-sixties, fewer letters for Kelly's secretaries to type, they had other jobs to keep them busy – such as checking the contents of the wine cellar and cataloguing the Japanese prints. The wine was mainly claret, including some of the finest vintages. In the Wine Book every bottle was named and listed as it was bought, laid down, and drunk. Mrs Reid recalls that before a dinner party 'Sir Gerald would decant some venerable bottle by means of a special wooden machine – a bottle cradle – which was slowly wound up so as to tip the bottle gently, all the while a light being projected at the neck to show up any movement of ullage.'

Down in the black cellar under Gloucester Place, the secretary would count dozens and dozens of bottles, to ascertain the accuracy of the Wine Book. It was worth taking trouble, for the claret proved an excellent investment. When he was 89, Kelly sold a lot of it for £3,700.

The Japanese prints that he retained into his old age were mostly facsimiles (earlier he owned a number of originals, most of which had been sold). He was over eighty when he asked guidance of Jack Hillier in sorting out the facsimiles and perhaps adding to this collection.

> The facsimiles are produced from woodblocks in the same manner as the originals [writes Mr Hillier] and have been published by Watanabe, Takimisawa, and other houses from say the 1920s onwards: Gerald had a pretty comprehensive collection, with some interesting groups of facsimiles of the same print by different publishers (and with some very strange and inexplicable differences sometimes!). He owned a large library of text-books on Japanese art. He confided rather shamefacedly that he did have a small number of *shunga* (the 'spring drawings' as erotica are called in Japan), and that he intended to leave them to the British Museum (which he did).

For Kelly's secretary, Mrs Reid, the Japanese prints meant long and rather heavy work, moving huge boxes about, trying to identify one subject from another, and typing lists of titles like 'Courtesan viewing lilies'; but she has on her walls 'two nicely framed prints by Utamaro – a present from G.F.K.'

'I left with regret of course,' she writes. 'I had been incredibly lucky to have established such a rapport . . . I used to go back for short visits in the next few years and he seemed only a little less ebullient. It would have been dreadful to witness any real decline in this original spirit.'

CHAPTER FIFTEEN

The Last Years

I

On reaching the age of 85, in April 1964, Kelly decided the time had come to resign as president of the Reynolds Club (the association of former students of the Royal Academy Schools). He took the trouble to compose a farewell speech, but left it in a taxi on the way to the annual dinner.

The next morning (6 May 1964), he wrote to Constance-Anne Parker, the club's treasurer, to apologize for any deficiencies in his oratory. He explained that, since his one-man show at the Academy in 1957, his pictures had been sent 'round and round the country until everybody is sick of them.' Now their travels had ended. 'Try and imagine the bother of finding places in the lower part of this house for over one hundred pictures without ruining my Studio . . . I was a very tired man when I came last night to your yearly dinner.'

The club had made him a present of one of his favourite wines, 'and of a good year'. Kelly said he would let the bottle settle down, and then drink their health.

'Nobody knows what the immediate future is going to bring to painting,' he told Miss Parker:

> It is quite obvious that modern pictures which certain people pretend to admire, can be produced by a painter who has had no training at all. Whether that is a good or a bad thing, they themselves will decide.
>
> Meanwhile, I hope that your Club continues to prosper, and that from time to time, you may think kindly of those who wish you well.

In his draft speech, Kelly said it was his great friend Sir Henry Rushbury, Keeper of the Royal Academy Schools, who had suggested he should be the first president of the Reynolds Club. 'This amazed me because he did not allow me into the school, on the grounds that I should depress the students and probably do them a lot of harm. However, I loved Henry and I did what he told me to do.'

The leave-taking, as Kelly wrote it – and as he probably contrived to express it without his typescript – was heart-warming, with a typical self-deprecatory twist:

> You look cheery enough, but then being a painter, or even a sculptor or even an architect, can be great fun. Painters have lots of good times! When I was young, I had a *lovely* time, and when I grew up, I went on having a *lovely* time. Everyone has been very kind to me, although I have not bothered to be very kind to them because I am, generally speaking, a very selfish old man.
>
> So, farewell to you all, and good luck!

2

In 1965, Somerset Maugham died. Like Kelly, he lived to be over ninety, but his final years were not without disturbance. Maugham attacked his wife Syrie in an autobiography published in America, quarrelled with his daughter, and adopted his secretary as his son.

The long friendship between Maugham and Kelly was untouched by the dark undercurrents in Maugham's life. 'Willie was a duck, an absolute duck,' said Kelly (*The Times*, 18 March 1969): 'A bit rum towards the end, mind you.' This succinct summary acknowledged that Kelly owed much to his friend. (Conversely, in earlier days, Kelly's companionship and enthusiasm for art had stimulated, even inspired Maugham.) And Kelly had shown his gratitude in a way that came instinctively to him – by becoming Maugham's principal portrait-painter (Plate 10a).

Kelly's loyalty to the past and to old friends was exceptionally strong. This extended, of course, to the work of artists who had particularly interested him. When the remarkable Aubrey Beardsley exhibition was held at the Victoria and Albert Museum in 1966, Kelly was invited to visit it privately, so that he could avoid the crowds. One evening, Brian Reade met him at the entrance shortly before closing time, and escorted him through the galleries.

The exhibition enchanted him [writes Mr Reade]: five rooms devoted mainly to the works of Beardsley, of whom he had been a great admirer, and what is more to the point, a distinguished collector. Again and again, indicating some of the most outstanding drawings in the exhibition, he was able to say, 'That used to belong to me.' They included The Kiss of Judas, The Abbé, Et in Arcadia Ego, The Lady with the Monkey, Volpone Adoring his Treasure, and several of the Lysistrata illustrations. He had acquired these in the earlier years of the century, but, so he told me, had been obliged to sell them later as he needed the money . . . How pleased he would be to know that I managed to get most of the Beardsley drawings he once owned into the Print Room at the V. and A. at the end of 1972.

3

Kelly used to say that Gloucester Place, having once been one of the quietest streets in London, had become one of the noisiest. In 1966 he asked the Noise Abatement Society to choose a painting of his to be sold for the society's benefit. (They chose a Burmese dancer painted in 1909.)

There are several legendary but unreliable stories about Kelly's independent behaviour on his own doorstep. Fully authentic, however, is a description by Renee Goldberg of how she became, in 1966, the last of Kelly's many secretaries:

When I came for my interview, I rang the door bell and an old man in a boiler suit answered the door. As it was many years since I had seen Sir Gerald on television – and then not in a boiler suit! – I was not sure whether this was Sir Gerald or not. I presumed that if he came in with me, he was Sir Gerald, and if not, then he would call for him.

However, he ushered me into the library, saying: 'Come in, come in – sit down,' so I presumed he was the great man himself. He looked me up and down and said 'You'll do – Do you think I will do? Come next Monday and we'll see how we get on,' and the next thing I knew was that I was back outside on the pavement.

That was my interview with Sir Gerald Kelly. Not a word about whether I could type or do shorthand, whether I had any references, or even whether I had ever been anybody's secretary before. I stayed with him until he died – $5\frac{1}{2}$ very interesting, often hectic, and really wonderful years.

He never knew my name, and only ever called me: 'I say.' So whenever I heard 'I say' I went running, like an obedient puppy.

When he felt very old and weary, he used to tell me that he thought he had lived too long, and I always told him not to say that, because then I would have to look for a new job. This always made him smile and he would say: 'All right then, I'll stay around a bit longer.'

There remained one more artistic crisis for Kelly to surmount – and it came as a sudden blow in a quarter where he was emotionally vulnerable. *The Sunday Times* of 1 January 1967, announced on its front page the 'biggest-ever art theft'. Three paintings by Rembrandt, three by Rubens, and others by Adam Elsheimer and Gerard Dou had been stolen on New Year's Eve from the Dulwich College Art Gallery. Kelly told *The Sunday Times*: 'It is a great shock to me. We didn't expect anything like this to happen.'

Fortunately the pictures were soon recovered; five of them were found under a bush on Streatham Common a few days later. On 3 March 1967, Kelly presided over a private view of the restored paintings, arranged to mark the re-opening of the gallery after repairs and reorganization. Television cameras were in action; Kelly made an appeal for funds to strengthen the gallery's defences. This and other appeals by him for the Dulwich Gallery had some success, but in 1971 the Gallery had to sell a picture to improve its finances.

Kelly, at 87, made a sprightly jesting figure, in his smart grey double-breasted suit, at the Dulwich press view. The stolen pictures had not been seriously damaged; but it was a good opportunity for Dr Hell to exercise his skill on them. They now looked better than ever. Rembrandt's portrait of Titus showed superb richness of colour and tone, and the cleaning had brought out Rembrandt's signature more clearly. Five of the pictures had new frames provided by Kelly.

Terry Coleman in the *Guardian* (4 March 1967) described Kelly as 'he prowled magnificently round the gallery' and 'had a brush or two with the teeming photographers'. At one point Kelly asked:

'Where's Hell?'

'What?'

'Where's Hell? Not the most promising name, I know, but he's the man.'

Dr Johann Hell, restorer of the eight slightly damaged pictures, was found, and they posed together in front of 'Girl at a Window'.

It was the happy culmination of a long and fruitful friendship.

4

With old age, Kelly did not lose his urge to travel. He and Jane visited
the Soviet Union when he was over eighty. Kelly told Colonel I. R.
Burrows (then military attaché at the Moscow Embassy) that his reason
for going to Leningrad was to see the Rembrandts at the Hermitage
Museum, that he had sat looking at each of them for an hour or more,
and that it had made his whole visit to Russia worth while. On his last
trip abroad, to Venice, he recorded the day's doings in a beautiful
handwriting that showed no deterioration.

His continuing vitality depended greatly on his ability to paint – not
of course at the old pressure, but still effectively. Kelly's portrait of
Lord Reith was hung in the 1967 Academy exhibition. One of the very
last portraits he painted was of Mrs Wylie McKissock, whose husband
had operated on him for neuralgia.

In the late summer of 1967, he and Jane were staying with friends on
the west coast of Scotland. They called one morning on a neighbour,
Mrs Valérie Spry. She found Kelly 'charming and friendly' but 'badly
bitten by the local midges'. He wrote to her on 22 September 1967:

> . . . I had heard of your house and garden and wanted to see
> it, although some sort of bug had made me look awful – much
> worse than usual.
>
> You kindly came forward with a tube of magical ointment which
> put me completely right. I am now very nearly as beautiful as I
> used to be!
>
> I enjoyed our visit and your garden is adorable. I have seen a lot
> of gardens in my time, but I have never seen so small a garden
> with so many novelties.

After an unsuccessful eye operation in his ninetieth year, Kelly could
no longer see to paint and told *The Times* (18 March 1969) that 'edges
have gone fuzzy'. He staved off boredom by reading Agatha Christie
novels with a special glass. *The Times* reporter found Kelly 'very much
on the ball', but henceforth life did lose some of its savour for him.
There is a parallel here with the concluding years of Sir Joshua Reynolds, though Reynolds was only 66 when he became half-blind.

Nancy Wise called to record an interview for the B.B.C. 'World at
One' programme, broadcast on Kelly's ninetieth birthday (9 April
1969). Mentioning that he had had a reputation for being outspoken,

even rumbustious, she asked whether he thought this had been a helpful device. Kelly responded characteristically:

> I've said what came into my head, I don't know why. I say, this
> is awfully dull, there's nothing you can say about me that's inter-
> esting. Don't . . . stop waving your head like that, I'm not an
> interesting man. Jane's very kind, she grins at me and says I'm a
> funny old thing, and lets me go at that, she's a very patient creature
> you know. I read Agatha Christie and I live a sensible sort of life.

Kelly declared he was not interested in the modern painting that was
being done, but that he would like to wander once again in his favourite
European cities: Florence, Rome, Paris, Seville, Madrid. Asked
whether he was pleased with his life, he answered:

> I've got through it . . . I've got through it. I've had very few
> illnesses. I think that painting in oils must be a very healthy occu-
> pation, because a great many of my fellow creatures who've painted
> lived to a great age. I suppose it's the turpentine or the linseed
> or something, you know, that they're breathing all the time. So
> you tell young painters that if there's nothing else they can get out
> of painting, they may have a long life.

The interviewer discovered that the Royal Academy was giving
Kelly a lunch on his ninetieth birthday. 'I expect he'll come back rather
tired and rather tiddly,' said Lady Kelly, laughing. Her husband
countered firmly: 'I'm entitled to be tired and I'm quite convinced I
shall not be tiddly.'

5

He enjoyed that Academy lunch, but convivial occasions now had to be
restricted. Edward Halliday was made a member of The Club in 1969,
and he tried to get Kelly to come to the dinners, offering to take him in
a car; but Jane said no to these invitations, feeling he was not quite up
to it. A last fully recognizable glimpse of Kelly in action derives from
his secretary, Mrs Goldberg, and belongs to the summer of 1969, when
Queen Elizabeth the Queen Mother was present at a garden party at the
Dulwich Gallery:

> Just as the Queen Mother was preparing to leave [writes Mrs
> Goldberg] it started to rain quite heavily and everybody had to

shelter. Sir Gerald, Lady Kelly and I were under the porch of the Gallery. The minute the rain stopped, Sir Gerald – in his usual impetuous manner – said 'Come on – we've been here long enough' and started walking quite briskly down the very long drive to the gates. When he had gone a little way, Lady Kelly asked me to bring him back because the Queen Mother would be leaving any minute, and as I went running after him, the band struck up 'God Save the Queen' and the Queen Mother started to leave, walking behind me; and by this time the drive was full of people on either side waiting to curtsy to the Queen Mother.

How I wished that the drive would open and swallow me up – I was so embarrassed; but when I finally caught up with Sir Gerald near the gates, he was quite oblivious of my embarrassment and just stayed to have another chat with the Queen Mother.

There is little to be recorded of the remaining two years of Kelly's life. Such a hard worker found it very trying to be idle; he could not paint, but he listened to music, and for as long as possible kept up his interests and his correspondence. To Mrs McClintock ('Miss Mansel') he wrote at Christmas, 1970: 'How nice of you to send us a card and such a pretty one. I hope you all have a very nice Christmas.' This was typewritten. Then came a few words in his own hand, which for the first time looked as if they had been written with difficulty: 'Come in & see us if you're passing. Gerald.'

He was fortunate in his friends; they did not fail him now. Kenneth Clark, Sir John Betjeman, Lord Adrian and many more cheered him by their visits.

In the end bronchial pneumonia set in, and Kelly died quietly and peacefully at his home on 5 January 1972, in his ninety-third year.

6

The funeral took place at Golders Green Crematorium on 7 January. A memorial service was held at St James's, Piccadilly, on 22 February, at which Sir Basil Spence read the lesson, and Sir Thomas Monnington, P.R.A., delivered a perceptive address. He began by saying that the distinguished congregation was there 'to recall and give thanks for the life and work of Gerald Festus Kelly', and he continued:

One way to do so might well be to sit quietly and think about that remarkable character. For my part, when I do so – and I have been thinking about him a great deal recently – I find his personality so strong that he is to all intents and purposes with me, and it is with no disrespect – rather the reverse – that I have to say that as usual he makes things rather difficult.

For I hear him saying: 'Sit here and think about me! I would have thought you could all find something better to do than that, but still, it is very kind of you to consider it.'

I have to confess: 'Well, actually, I was going to *say* something about you.'

'Oh,' he seems to say, 'I can't see much point in that – after all, most of the people here knew me, or they would not be here. They will not want to hear you blathering about me. Anyway, what were you going to say?'

That would be typical, for although he had no time for nonsense, he was usually prepared to listen, in case anyone might have something sensible to say.

I don't know whether he would think it sense if I say: men create their own memorial, through their human relationships, and, if they happen to be creative, through what they create.

Monnington went on to do justice to Kelly as a painter, a friend of painters, and a great President of the Royal Academy. 'The Academy had and has every reason to be grateful to Sir Gerald for his achievement during the five years of his Presidency. The Academy also had reason to be grateful for his television appearances, when his enthusiasm in front of the camera became infectious and brought thousands to the Galleries. . . .' Nor did he forget Kelly's work for Dulwich.

A memorial tablet designed by David McFall, R.A., was unveiled by Sir Thomas Monnington in the crypt of St Paul's Cathedral on 22 November 1973. Kelly is therefore commemorated near the grave of Sir Joshua Reynolds – to whom a writer inevitably returns for a general comparison between two notably effective but very different Presidents. In one respect they were entirely in accord. Both were happiest working in their studios. Both found the art of painting 'beyond all others'; and Kelly would have echoed Sir Joshua's smiling confession to Boswell – made in the last weeks of his life – that he had 'indeed indulged that notion all along'.

Some Works by Gerald Kelly in Public and Semi-public Collections in Great Britain and Eire

(Oil on canvas unless otherwise stated; measurements in inches.)

CAMBRIDGE

Jesus College: Charles Whibley (28 × 25½)
Pembroke College: H. G. Comber (34½ × 29½)
Trinity Hall:
   Dr Henry Bond (36 × 30)
   Frederic, Viscount Maugham, Lord High Chancellor (53½ × 34½)
University Registry: Dr J. N. Keynes (33 × 36)

CORK

Art Gallery: Sasha Kropotkin Lebedeff (30 × 25)

DUBLIN

Municipal Gallery of Modern Art:
   Mrs Harrison (68 × 29½)
   Frank Rutter (32 × 25½)
   At the Stage Door (70 × 33½)

ETON COLLEGE

College Hall: Dr M. R. James, O.M. (57 × 40¼)
Art Collection: Upper School, Eton, after the bombing, December 1940
   (16¼ × 13, oil on paper)

GLASGOW

Art Gallery and Museum: The Blue Door (Consuelo VIII) (50 × 30)

HULL

Ferens Art Gallery: The Countess of Lisburne (40¼ × 45¼)

LONDON

British Museum: Sir John Forsdyke (30 × 25)
Garrick Club: Arthur Bourchier as Long John Silver (79 × 40)
National Liberal Club: Sir John Simon, Chancellor of the Exchequer (50 × 40)
Royal Academy of Arts:
　Jane XXX, Diploma Work (29½ × 24½)
　Posthumous Portrait of H.M. King George VI (49 × 32)
Royal College of Music:
　Dr Ralph Vaughan Williams, O.M. (35 × 45)
　Sir Malcolm Sargent (53¼ × 35¾)
St Mary's Hospital: Wright-Fleming Institute of Microbiology: Sir Almroth Wright
　(37 × 42)
Tate Gallery:
　The Vicar in his Study, the artist's father (46 × 37½)
　Ma Si Gyaw IV (50 × 40)
　The Jester (W. Somerset Maugham) (40 × 30)
Westfield College: Dr Eleanor C. Lodge (30 × 25)

TRURO

Art Gallery: George D. Hornblower (44 × 47¾)

WINDSOR CASTLE

　King George VI: The State Portrait (108 × 68)
　Queen Elizabeth: The State Portrait (107 × 70)

Bibliography

Artist, The, 'Famous Artists: Gerald Kelly, R.A.', by the Editor (June 1932)

Bell, Clive, *Old Friends: Personal Recollections* (1956)

Bennett, Arnold, *Journals: 1896–1910*, ed. Newman Flower (1932)

Bodkin, Thomas, *Hugh Lane and his Pictures* (3rd edn, Dublin 1956)

Bond, Henry, *A History of the Trinity Hall Boat Club* (1930)

Cordell, Richard, *Somerset Maugham: A Biographical and Critical Study* (1961)

Catalogue of Exhibition of Works by Sir Gerald Kelly, K.C.V.O., P.P.R.A. (Royal Academy of Arts 1957)

Crowley, Aleister, *The Confessions of Aleister Crowley: An Autohagiography*, ed. John Symonds and Kenneth Grant (1969)

Eton College Register, Part VI, 1889–1899

Gilmore, Tamara, *Me and My American Husband* (New York 1968)

Gregory, Lady, *Hugh Lane's Life and Achievement, with some Account of the Dublin Galleries* (1921)

Hart-Davis, Rupert, *Hugh Walpole: A Biography* (1952)

Heygate, Elizabeth, *A Girl at Eton* (1965)

Hone, William, *The Life of Henry Tonks* (1939)

Hudson, Derek, *James Pryde* (1949)

  Sir Joshua Reynolds (1958)

Hutchison, Sidney C., *The History of the Royal Academy 1768–1968* (1968)

Léautaud, Paul, *Journal Littéraire*, Vol. I, 1893–1906 (Paris 1954)

  Journal Littéraire, Vol. XII, 1937–1940 (Paris 1962)

  Journal of a Man of Letters, 1898–1907, trans. Geoffrey Sainsbury (London 1960)

Maugham, W. Somerset, 'A Student of Character: Gerald Festus Kelly', *International Studio* (January 1915)

  Of Human Bondage (1915)

  Ashenden (1928)

  Cakes and Ale (1930)

  The Magician 'with a fragment of autobiography' (collected edn, 1956)

  Purely for my Pleasure (1962)

Munnings, Sir Alfred, *The Second Burst* (1951)

  The Finish (1952)

Nicolson, Harold, *Diaries and Letters 1945–1962* (1968)

Nicolson, Nigel, *The Life of Field Marshal Earl Alexander of Tunis* (1973)

Pound, Reginald, *The Englishman: A Biography of Sir Alfred Munnings* (1962)

Roberts, Cecil, *The Pleasant Years* (1974)

Rothenstein, Sir John, *Brave Day Hideous Night: Autobiography 1939–1965* (1966)

Sotheby's Sales Catalogues, 18 November, 7 December, 14 December 1955

Symonds, John, *The Great Beast: The Life and Magick of Aleister Crowley* (1971)

Tate Gallery Catalogue, 'The Modern British Paintings, Drawings, and Sculpture', Vol. I, by Mary Chamot, Dennis Farr and Martin Butlin (1964)

Toye, Francis, *For What We Have Received: An Autobiography* (1950)

Truly Thankful? A Sequel to an Autobiography (1957)

Venn, J. A. (compiler), *Alumni Cantabrigienses*, Part II: 1752–1900 (1951)

Notes on Sources

Principal sources have been:

(1) Sir Gerald Kelly's private papers containing letters addressed to him, copies of letters written by him, and press cuttings;

(2) the files of the Royal Academy of Arts which hold letters addressed to him, copies of his own letters, press cuttings, and official transcripts of speeches made at Academy banquets;

(3) B.B.C. transcripts of radio and television broadcasts, belonging to Lady Kelly.

I have been indebted not only to Lady Kelly's recollections but to the many letters written to me by Kelly's friends, acquaintances, sitters, secretaries, and assistants, whom I have thanked in my preface. They in turn have often communicated to me letters written to them by Kelly. In general, I have acknowledged sources, including newspapers, in the text, with dates wherever possible. In the bibliography and the following explanatory notes on individual chapters readers will be able to trace other sources.

CHAPTER 1: ANCESTRY AND EDUCATION

Burke's Landed Gentry (1952), 'Kelly of Leesthorpe Hall'; a booklet *1799–1899 Centenary of the Post Office London Directory*; information from the secretary of Kelly's Directories; *Eton College Register*; Venn's *Alumni Cantabrigienses*. For Trinity Hall: Bond's History of the Trinity Hall Boat Club and information from Graham Storey. For Crowley: biography by John Symonds, and *Confessions*, ed. Symonds and Grant.

CHAPTER 2: ARRIVAL IN PARIS

B.B.C. transcripts of television recordings made for *Sir Gerald Kelly Remembers* (1956) are the principal source.

CHAPTER 3: THE 'CHAT BLANC'

B.B.C. television transcripts; diaries of Paul Léautaud and Arnold Bennett; *Old Friends* by Clive Bell, and recollections by W. S. Maugham prefaced to 1956 edition of *The Magician*; books on Hugh Lane by Lady Gregory and

Thomas Bodkin. There are letters from Crowley to Kelly among the Crowley Papers, Warburg Institute, University of London.

CHAPTER 4: MAUGHAM'S FRIEND

The literary executor of W. Somerset Maugham having allowed a limited use of Maugham's many letters to Kelly, these have proved an important source of information for this period.

CHAPTER 5: FASHIONABLE PORTRAIT-PAINTER

It is due to Dr L. Holliday that I have been able to say something about Kelly's friendship with Alan Beeton. Dr Frederick W. Hilles of Yale kept the illuminating diary of 1930–31 which he has allowed me to quote. Kelly's letters to W. H. Riddell were contributed by the Marqués de Saavedra.

CHAPTER 6: THE STATE PORTRAITS

This chapter and the next owe much to the recollections and assistance of Sir Owen Morshead. For Kelly's letter to Munnings on the latter's election as P.R.A., see R. Pound's biography of Munnings, *The Englishman*. Mr E. C. Shaw of Dulwich College described for me the scope of Kelly's work for the Dulwich Gallery.

CHAPTER 7: THE GREAT CLEANING CONTROVERSY

Kelly's letter to Munnings of 8 February 1949 is published in R. Pound, *The Englishman*.

CHAPTER 8: THE PRESIDENT

This and the next four chapters are largely based on the R.A. files. For Munnings on Spencer, see R. Pound, *The Englishman*.

CHAPTER 9: EXHIBITIONS AT BURLINGTON HOUSE

Churchill's letter to Kelly of 16 March 1952, is among Kelly's personal papers; Churchill's other letters to him and copies of some of Kelly's letters to Churchill are in R.A. files. Kelly's letter to Brangwyn of 26 August 1952, together with a considerable correspondence between Kelly and Count William de Belleroche and his mother, have been supplied by Mr Gordon P. Anderson.

CHAPTER 10: TELEVISION STAR

Mr Cecil Roberts showed me Kelly's letter to him of 13 August 1952, before it appeared in his book, *The Pleasant Years* (1974). Mr Oliver Davies, Keeper of Portraits at the Royal College of Music, drew attention to Kelly's account of how he painted Ralph Vaughan Williams, and made available the correspondence between Kelly and the R.C.M. The description of Kelly's first television broadcast is based largely on the recollections of Bill Duncalf and Edward Halliday.

CHAPTER 14: AN INDOMITABLE PAINTER

Kelly's letter to Lionel Edwards of 21 July 1959, after the death of Munnings, is taken from his secretary's copy.

Index

Also by Derek Hudson

HOLLAND HOUSE IN KENSINGTON

The garden, park and a small part of the structure of Holland House remain today, and the author has succeeded in making this great house live again, not in static details of its architectural features but in terms of the full-blooded social history that was created within its shelter. A fascinating text and exceptional illustrations make this a book for lasting pleasure.

'Macaulay would surely have approved of Derek Hudson's book. Excellently produced pictures and plans go well with his text.'

The Times

'Mr Hudson writes sensitively and engagingly about the occupants of the house, their friends, and associations, and the range of their opinions and preoccupations.'

Asa Briggs: *Yorkshire Post*

'It is good to be reminded so pleasantly and with such well-selected detail, of the comings and goings of a long-past age of politics and literature . . . Armed with the information offered by this book, the most casual visitor will be able to appreciate why, and for so long a span, it attracted so much of what was sparkling in the life of its time.'

Oliver Warner: *The Daily Telegraph*